WITNESS

MEMOIR OF
W. ALVIN JACKSON

First Edition

ISBN 978-0-578-07713-0

Library of Congress Control number: 2011901152

AUTHOR'S NOTE: The depiction of individuals and descriptions of events in this book are based on the recollections and memories of the author as well as his perspective. Others present during these events may have a different recollection or perspective. The biblical references and scriptures are primarily from the New International Version bible.

Printed in the United States

Cover Design by Alyssa B. Jackson

Editing by Judith Gitenstein – Editorial Services

Proofreading by Jon R. Kaufmann – Kaufmann Proofing Services

DEDICATION

Elnora Jackson

This book is dedicated to my mother, Elnora Jackson, who paved the way for my journey; to my wife, Rita Jackson, who has been by my side through the good and bad times; and to my children, Richard, Alyssa and Danielle, who have made the ride a lot more interesting and worthwhile.

ACKNOWLEDGEMENTS

This book could not have been written if not for all the support I received from my friends and family. Most importantly, the road I traveled and the great people I met along the way who shaped and influenced my life would not have been possible if not for the presence of God.

During economically challenging times, the call to eliminate federal funding for community-based programs, especially those geared toward the disadvantaged, continues to rise. While it is understandable, given the need to reduce the overall level of government spending, the impact of doing so could be catastrophic for underserved communities. I cannot begin to imagine what would have become of my life, if not for programs like the NYC (Neighborhood Youth Corporation). The NYC provided me with my first real part-time job and paycheck while I was in high school. Nor can I begin to think about the long, hot and penniless summers without the Urban League helping me find work.

The desire and thirst for getting a good education, instilled in me by my mother, was fueled by federally funded programs. It was a government program that allowed me to travel to Wheaton College every Wednesday to be tutored. "The Education for Life Program" at The Firman House, which I attended every Tuesday, introduced me to professionals who shared their life stories and provided me and 52 other students with the trip of our lives. It was the Upward Bound Program at Loyola University of Chicago that prepared me for college and the challenges of living away from home for the first time.

Any acknowledgement for me would not be complete without recognizing the special men in my life who acted as role models, mentors and surrogate fathers. I extend my deepest gratitude and appreciation to Dr. Anderson Thompson, Dr. Thaddeus Kostrubala, Eugene Bogan, William Finch, Dr. Harold Pace, Alvin Lubov, Dr. Barney Berlin, William H. Adkins and John H. Johnson.

I would like to give special thanks to one of my colleagues - Dr. Phares Noel II, who continued to encourage, prod and insist that I write this book. I also want to thank God for Rev. Troy Benton for being my spiritual guide as I tried to make sense out of the journey I have traveled and witnessed. Lastly, I want to pay a special tribute to my cousins Anthony Cole and Josiah Curry, who I have come to have the same close relationship with that our parents shared.

TABLE OF CONTENT

TABLE OF CONTENT

FOREWORD

The title of this book, *Witness,* represents what is often referred to as a double entendre - having a double meaning. On the surface, the book reveals and describes in great detail events in my life that have shaped the person I am today. Beneath the surface, on a spiritual level, it allows me to "give witness" (publicly acknowledge) the presence of God in my life and the journey it has taken me on. In most Baptist and some Methodist churches, worshipers overwhelmed with emotion stemming from the realization of His goodness and grace stand, shout and give praise, or as my elders would say, "testify" or witness. In this book, I will do neither; instead I will highlight and point out those times when, in the words of the great gospel singer, Mahalia Jackson "My Soul Looks Back and Wonders How I Got Over."

Throughout my entire life, I have struggled with understanding what "God's perfect will" is for me and how you square that with your own dreams and desires. I have often asked myself the question "When does His perfect will begin and one's free will end, or is free will just a fallacy?" Too many times I have created the perfect plan and executed it flawlessly, only to have it end in disaster. Then there have been countless times when things in complete and utter chaos have come together miraculously, in a way far greater than I could have imagined. There are also those occasions when I have prayed for a miracle and nothing happened and times when I have questioned how God could let that happen.

The writing of this book has afforded me the opportunity to take a long, hard look at my life and to acknowledge the times when it is obvious that

His perfect will has been at play in my life. It will also permit me a chance to better understand many of the lessons He has tried to teach me.

I embark upon this endeavor with the hope that you will be entertained and that you and I will find answers for many of the unanswered questions we have struggled with most of our lives.

Your Witness in Chief

CHAPTER 1

THE STRUGGLE TO SURVIVE

Even the Orphans Seemed to Have More

In the U.S., it is common knowledge that children raised by a single parent grow up with fewer financial and educational advantages than children reared in a home with both parents. According to a report published in 2004 by the Single Parent Success Foundation, births to unmarried women reached 36 percent of total births, accounting for approximately 1.5 million births that year. More than half of these births were to women in their early twenties and another 30 percent to single women between the ages of 25 - 29. The latest U.S. Census Report shows that in 2008, 41 percent of births were to unmarried women, up from 40 percent in 2007.

Approximately, 60 percent of children living with single mothers in 1995 were near the poverty line, and it is doubtful we have seen any improvements. According to a recent report from the Associated Press 72 percent of African-American babies are born out of wedlock. There is no question that the odds of success were stacked high against an African-American male child raised by a single parent in the '50s on the South Side of Chicago, which is where my story begins.

The 1950s were marked by the Korean War, the beginning of the mass production of computers, the introduction of credit cards, and the launch of color TVs, the beginning of the rock 'n' roll" era and the election of Dwight D. Eisenhower as President of the United States in 1952. That same year Salk polio vaccines were used for the first time to protect children against polio. Five years later (in 1957) the Russians launched Sputnik, the first satellite to orbit the earth. The following year came the great switch from 45s to stereo LP records. One year later Fidel Castro took power in Cuba and became the new dictator. Throughout the '50s American families continued to prosper; in fact, 54 percent of American homes had a TV set, and the annual family income reached $5,000.

Chicago, the city where I was born on September, 20, 1950 was and is still today a bustling town. In the '50s it was known for many things such as its slaughterhouses, steel mill, financial district, top-rated universities and colleges and great shopping. It was also known back then for its skyscrapers, lakefront, and highly developed mass transit system and without question its strong ethnicity and hard-charging politics. It was an industrial town with plenty of manufacturing and service-related jobs available. Many Blacks from the South moved to Chicago in what has become known as the Great Migration, in search of higher paying jobs and a better quality of life. Besides the cold and often brutal winter weather, what they found was a city filled with ethnicity that dictated where you lived.

Blacks lived either on the South Side (where most arrived on the train at the 26th Street Station) or later on the West Side. The low end of the South Side was characterized by its large apartment buildings and never ending brownstones. The farther south you went (71st and beyond), the nicer and more affluent the communities and the more single-family homes you would find.

Throughout the South Side were major thoroughfares called streets running east and west. These streets were where all the action/commerce took place from shopping, eating and hustling to drinking, partying and catching the EL (the rapid transit system). The major streets on the Southside were 35th, 39th, 43rd, 47th, 51st, 55th, 61st, 63rd, 71st, 75th, 79th, 83rd, 87th and 95th Street.

North Avenue from Wells Street to Harlem Avenue and the entire near North Side was where the Italians lived. The area was filled with excellent restaurants, markets and merchants of Italian descent selling everything Italian. They also had a heavy presence in suburban communities like

2

Schiller Park, River Forest, Franklin Park and Rosemont and later in places in DuPage County like Bensenville, Wheaton and Elmhurst. They controlled the jobs in the Streets and Sanitation Department as well as the State of Illinois Highway Department.

One of the best-known and most popular sections in Chicago was Maxwell Street, the center of Jewish commerce. You could buy anything in what was affectionately (from our side at least) called "Jew-Town." The merchants would line the streets, selling everything from clothing items to household goods. Every visit was topped off with the purchase of a Polish sausage or hot dog with grilled onions and a pop (soft drink). On Saturdays and Sundays, it was so crowded you could barely make your way through the streets. While many of the Jewish community members operated businesses in the Maxwell Street area, most did not live there. They lived in many of the more affluent areas such as Rogers Park, Lake Shore Drive, Hyde Park, Park Ridge, Skokie and Lincolnwood.

Other ethnic groups like the Czechs lived along Cermak Road (22nd Street), around Cicero and Berwyn. Polish Americans lived in what was called "Six Corners" the area where Milwaukee Avenue crosses Cicero Avenue. The Germans lived in a small neighborhood on Lincoln near Belmont and Ashland. The Greeks were concentrated on Halsted Street, south of Randolph Street. The Irish (and there were plenty of Irish-Americans in Chicago, including the Mayor Daley family), lived on the South Side, in an area west of where many Blacks lived, near the "Back of the Yards"" area. There was a railroad track that separated the two groups. If you were Black and lived near this area you knew never to cross the tracks for fear of being beaten up or worse.

We lived on Lake Park. To be exact, the address was 3603 South Lake Park. I hesitate to call it an apartment building, because most of the units in the building were not apartments. The majority of them did not have a living

3

room, dining room or separate kitchen or bedroom area. The building had three floors plus a basement. It was made up of mostly one-room units with a small area for cooking and no bathroom. The bathroom was located in the hall and shared by all the families that lived on the floor, which could be anywhere from three to four. In fact, the first place I can recall living in was just that - one room with a tiny kitchen area on the first floor. It housed my mother, Elnora Jackson (age 30), and my sister, Shirley Jackson (affectionately referred to as Baby Sister), who was two years older than me and my older brother, Isaac Barlow, known as Little Barlow, who was four years older than I.

The neighborhood consisted of other buildings similar to ours, a few large apartment buildings and several two-to three-family brownstones directly across the street from us.

The two most notable things about the neighborhood was that immediately to the east of the building was the Illinois Central (IC) railroad tracks, South Lake Shore Drive and a small park that butted up to Lake Michigan. The other noteworthy thing was that three buildings to the north was a large walled-in complex where orphans lived. To this day, I do not know the name or religious affiliation of the orphanage. What I do remember is envying them because I thought they were better off. They had lots of toys (more than we had), a nice place to play (albeit behind the walls) and plenty to eat. They also didn't seem to have to struggle every day the way we did.

My building, 3603 South Lake Park, and the surrounding neighborhood was filled with tight-knit families and interesting characters. The Dunigan family lived in our building and was like royalty. There was Bill Dunigan a tall light-skinned likeable man who always drove the latest Cadillac and had an eye for the ladies. He seemed to be everywhere: he was the janitor for

4

several of the buildings in the neighborhood, including ours. He also worked full-time as the janitor for some school or company. Money did not seem to be a problem for him or his family. His wife (Fannie Dunigan) was a darker-skinned woman who dressed exceptionally well. She was heavily involved in her church, West Point Missionary Baptist Church.

Bill and Fannie Dunigan had two older children, a son everybody called Sonny and a daughter we knew as Bootsey. When Sonny married Diane, a gorgeous young lady with dyed platinum blonde hair, it was truly a royal wedding. They rode in a brand new Buick and received a bunch of nice gifts. The reason I know this is that oftentimes I played with Sonny's nephews Cleveland and Stephen (Lefty and Bootsey's children). They were about my age and often came to visit their grandparents. During one of those visits, we were upstairs, and I saw all the gifts.

Sonny and Diane moved into one of the units on the second floor after they got married. Another family that lived in the building on the second floor was the Williams. The family included Mr. and Mrs. Williams and their two daughters, Karen and Yvonne. Karen was close to my age, and Yvonne was about my sister's age. They were a nice and cordial family that everybody got along with. There was also an older lady in the building on the third floor named Miss Irene. She was related to the Dunigans. I don't remember much about her except that on Halloween, she would never give you candy. Instead, she would always play a prank on you.

We also had another family that lived on the first floor in the front unit, a husband and wife and two small children. One of the children was Bubba, who would eat my marbles if I didn't snatch them away from him before he had a chance to put them in his mouth.

Besides the families in the building, we had a few very interesting characters who lived at 3603 or visited relatives there. High on the list was a man named Mr. Rock, who was a resident of the building. He was a tall and thin Creole from New Orleans. He had long black curly hair and a goatee, and played the guitar. He drove a sky blue Pontiac convertible and loved to keep up foolishness with the women. I am not sure what he did for a living. I think he was a musician. What I do know is that he was funny and a real character. He would tell the story about how one night Mr. Dunigan went to one of the tenants to ask them to keep the noise down. This particular tenant would hold card parties in their unit. Besides the complaints from the other tenant about the noise, I don't think Mrs. Dunigan liked the fact that they were gambling in the building. According to Mr. Rock, when Mr. Dunigan went to ask them nicely to keep the noise down, they got smart with him. Mr. Rock described what happened after that. He said "Mista Dunigan didn't arga with'em, he just left and come back wit the biggest gun I'd ever seen. Man that gun was so big it had wheels on it and when them folks saw dat gun ever'body went to runnin, cluding the rats and roaches." You see, back then you didn't have to go to court to evict a tenant. You just threw them out.

Alex Williams, the uncle of Karen and Yvonne, was another character. He drove a Studebaker and was always in and out of the building. He was known for being a big liar and unbeknownst to us, he was also a thief. One day my mother had to run errands and asked him if he would watch us, since we were playing with his nieces. He said sure and she left. Before doing so, she told him she was going to leave the door to our unit cracked just in case we needed something from inside. A few days later, she was looking for her Plaid Stamps books. She was planning on redeeming them for something she had seen in the Plaid Stamps catalog. She searched high and low and could not find them. She reasoned that some how, one of us was playing with them and misplaced them. Of course, we got a whopping which during those times was the norm when you misbehaved. It wasn't until several weeks later, while talking to Mrs. Williams, that she learned that her brother-in-law Alex gave them a bunch of nice gifts he got from redeeming his Plaid Stamp books. My mother didn't think for a second that it was a coincidence and knew it was Alex, who had stolen her stamps. We, on the other hand, hated him because he caused us to get a serious whopping for something we didn't do. We sought revenge and got it one day when we saw him driving up to the building. We knew from conversations with Karen and Yvonne that he was coming to visit. We waited patiently for him at the window in the hallway on the third floor. When he pulled up with the top down on his car, we let him have it with raw eggs we had stolen from the refrigerator. As hard as food was to come by oddly enough we did not get a whopping.

Living in our building in the basement were Miss Idella and Mr. Edward. Mr. Edward was a small thin man and Miss Idella was a large buxom woman who loved to walk around barefoot. In the summer, she would sit on the front porch with her skirt draped between her legs, fanning. She and Mr. Edward fought constantly and one night, she chased him out of the back door of the building with a butcher's knife in her hand. He jumped the wall behind the building and headed for the IC (Illinois Central) railroad tracks. Before reaching the tracks, he pleaded with her to calm down and put away the knife. She refused to do so until finally Mrs. Dunigan came out and said, "Idella have you lost your mind? Put down that knife and let that man come home so that we can all get some sleep."

When Mrs. Dunigan, who on the surface appeared to do no wrong and was a church going Christian, asked you to do something you did it. Miss. Idella replied "Yes, ma'am" and she and Edward returned to their unit without another cross word being said.

7

In the building to the north of us lived Plucom and Jerry. They were two brothers who I played with a lot. Plucom was close to my age, and Jerry was a little older. They lived with their parents in a building I think was owned or managed by their grandparents. They were rough and tumble, and most of the adults described them as being "bad" kids. I got into trouble most of the times when I played with them. Once they talked me into pulling the fire alarm, and we got into trouble.

Plucom and Jerry lived right next door to the orphanage. We could see directly into the orphanage from the windows in their apartment. I would be visiting, watching them make their infamous sugar sandwiches, plotting how we were going to jump over the wall and steal some of the toys we saw lying around in the yard. They had plenty of toys, including brand-new bikes.

Now back to the sugar sandwiches: they would take white bread and smear it with butter and sprinkle sugar on top and then eat it. I never acquired a taste for the delicacy and instead would have a peanut butter and jelly sandwich when I visited, provided of course they had peanut butter and jelly, which oftentimes they didn't.

While we never stole any of the bikes because they would be too hard to hide, we did steal other toys from them. I can recall our getting caught once or twice and receiving the beating of our lives from our parents because they could not understand why we would steal from poor little orphans.

One other person I often played with was Huck. He lived in the building south of us with his parents, Mr. & Mrs. Wiley, and two older brothers, Barney and Calvin (Little Wash). It was the same building where Mr. Frank (my barber) lived in the basement and where I got my hair cut. When I played with Huck, I was less likely to get into trouble. He was more the adventuresome type that liked exploring and building things. We would build scooters, top shooters and tree houses in the backyard. We would always explore the area behind the building right before the IC tracks.

At the end of our backyard was a brick wall about two feet tall. If you jumped over the wall to the other side, which was about a five-foot drop, you would end up in a tall grassy area that led up to the IC tracks. People tossed all kinds of things back there and for us, it was like Treasure Island. We could find all sorts of things, most of which were of little value to anyone other than us. Huck and I spent a lot of time together because his mother, Mrs. Wiley, was good friends with my mother. My older brother Barlow also played with his Huck's older brothers.

Another kid I played with frequently was Earl. He lived in the same building as the Wileys. His father's name was Benny C and I can't remember his mom's name. He had an older sister and two brothers. His younger brother was Jerome, and his older one was Willy C. They were related to the Dunigans, possibly cousins. Benny C was a drinker like many of the men in the neighborhood. He was always telling jokes and was very playful. He would tickle you or grab you by the head and take his knuckle and drill it into your head. He was always the life of the party.

Earl was less of a joker and more of a go-getter like me. We were known for always looking for work that would pay us a nickel, dime or quarter. We would go to the store for you or take out your garbage. We also went from house to house looking for bottles that we could return to the store for the two-cent deposit. Earl and I would go to the grocery store (Mr. Fletcher's) and the meat market on 36th street on the corners of Ellis and Cottage Grove looking for women, we could convince to let us carry their grocery home. Bill Cook, the brother of the legendary crooner Sam

Cook (whose professional name became Sam Cooke), worked at the meat market and would attest to our being good kids.

There was only one girl in the neighborhood that I played with. Her name was Regina Jordan. She lived in the big courtway building with her mom and dad, next door to Huck and Earl. Everyone in that building seemed to have money. Most of the families had nice apartments with living room and bedroom furniture sets like the ones you saw in the furniture stores. In fact, Regina's parents were the first family on the block that I can recall having a color TV. Regina also had an aunt who lived in the building. She was single and very pretty. She gave my mom nice things for my sister Shirley.

One of my best customers was Miss Cissy who lived in the court way building. At least once or twice a week she would get the word to me that she needed me to go to the store for her. There was also Mr. and Mrs. Fine. I think Mr. Fine worked on the railroad as a Pullman porter and was gone most of the time. When he was home, he drove a big black shiny Chrysler.

The Cates' were another prominent family that resided in the courtway building. The patriarch and matriarch of the family were BB and Hazel Cates. Everyone called Mrs. Hazel "Big Hazel" because she had a daughter who lived in the building that we called "Little Hazel." BB and Big Hazel were from New Orleans and loved making a big pot of gumbo and inviting everybody over.

I think BB was a railroad man, and Big Hazel wrote "policy." Policy was betting on the numbers (similar to the lottery) except that it was not government sponsored or run. This made Big Hazel a great customer for me. I was either being directed by her to go pick up the numbers from one of her customers or receiving a message from them to come get their numbers. Their daughter, Little Hazel, had what was called a French basement apartment in the building. In the early years, she was buck wild and flirtatious. She teased and taunted the men and boys in the neighborhood, young and old. Even though she was at least five years older than my brother (Barlow) I think she was his first sexual encounter. She eventually settled down (or so we thought) and married a musician named Ray, who played the guitar. Their relationship was tumultuous most of the time and continued that way after having two children, Ray Jr. and a daughter named Patricia.

In addition to my friends, I sometimes played with my sister's friends. It was more a matter of convenience than choice. Since she was often relegated to watch me, I ended up playing with them. That included hanging out with her and the Hickman girls, Rosie, Peaches and Cookie. Peaches was my sister's age, and I think Rosie was my age. They lived down the street from us, close to 35th Street directly across from the orphanage in a brownstone with a tall flight of steps leading to their front door. Their parents Mr. and Mrs. Hickman were nice people. He played the bass in a band. It was funny watching him carry the bass. He was short and round in the middle and so was the bass. When we played with them Peaches always wanted to play house. Since I was the only male in the group I was always cast in the role of the dad/husband with Peaches being the mom. She took her role seriously and made sure we did everything that moms and dads did.

Three doors down from the Hickmans were the Welches. Mr. Welch whom everyone called "Tootsie," was Benny C's brother. He and his wife had two daughters, Augustella and Jeannie. My sister played with them and of course dragged me along. Augustella was more like a big sister to Shirley, and Jeannie was a little younger than me. Like his brother, Tootsie

11

loved to drink and was very playful. His wife, on the other hand, always appeared to be sickly.

My mother, who was called Mrs. Barlow, had a lot of girlfriends in the neighborhood, which was especially tough on me. It meant that if any of them caught me miss-behaving they had her permission to whop me. They would also tell her, causing me to get another whopping when she came home.

They called my mom Mrs. Barlow because that was the last name of Isaac and Shirley's father, James Barlow. While they were never married they were together for a long time, and she worked as a waitress or cook in several restaurants that he managed and/or owned. I will talk more about their relationship later. One of her girlfriends was Mrs. Stroger. She lived across the street from us with her husband. They had one son who died relatively young. She was my mother's confidant. She was a tall good-looking brown-skinned woman known throughout the neighborhood for not taking any mess off anyone.

Mrs. Rosetta Walker, who was married to Mr. Charles and the mother of John Henry and Butch Walker, was her church going girlfriend. She was a fast-talking, short, high-energy woman who attended church several times a week. She was sort of my mother's spiritual advisor, whereas Mrs. Stroger gave her advice on men, which my mother badly needed. Miss Rosetta encouraged her to go to her church and sometimes would take us along. She must have been a nurse at the church. I remember her wearing a white uniform with matching white shoes and stockings and a little white hat with a blue cape and pocket hanky. Much later in life they would become ushers together at Fellowship Missionary Baptist Church.

The other family that was close to us and another one of my mother's girlfriends was Mrs. Shane. She had a son named Sonny and a daughter called Dorothy Jean, who babysat all three of us. She was about ten years older than my brother Barlow. I have a vague memory of there being a Mr. Shane, but I am not certain. What I remember most about them is that they took me on my first and only trip to the South, to Alabama. I had never been out of the city or on a Greyhound Bus until I went south with them.

The last family I want to introduce to you are the Cheatams. I know there were a mom and dad and at least two children but can't remember much more about them. The only one that I can vividly remember is Sammie Cheatam. He was called "Noonie." He was very tall and went around the building singing gospel songs all the time. His mannerisms were different and he didn't talk like the other teenage boys his age. He was much older than we were and my mom would occasionally have him baby sit us.

#

Throughout this early part of my life, I was oblivious to God. I learned of Him when I went to Sunday school at West Point Missionary Baptist Church. I knew that it was important to go to church and to try to be a good Christian. Beyond that I had no clue of what it meant to have a relationship with God or how you went about doing it. Most of my early childhood was spent envying others.

In accordance with 1 Peters 2, what I did not understand at the time was that I needed to put away my feelings of envy and jealousy; and like a newborn long for spiritual substance so that I can grow into salvation provided of course I know the Lord. As we come to Him rejected by man but in God's sight chosen and precious we are like living stones being used to build a spiritual house that will become a priesthood offering spiritual sacrifices acceptable to God through Jesus Christ. The scripture says:

"Behold, I am laying in Zion a stone, a cornerstone chosen and precious and whosoever believes in Him will not be put to shame." The honor is for those who believe; non-believers the rejected cornerstones the builders use will falter and be offensive. They will do so because they disobey the word as they were destined to do.

As believers we are a chosen race, a royal priesthood, a holy nation, a people for His own possession, that you may proclaim the excellences of Him who called us out of darkness into His marvelous light. Once we were not a people, but now we are God's people; once we had not received mercy, but now we have received mercy. He urges His beloved, as sojourners and exiles to abstain from the passions of the flesh, which wage war against the soul. To keep your conduct among the Gentiles honorable, so that when they speak against you as evildoers, they may see your good deeds and glorify God on the day of visitation.

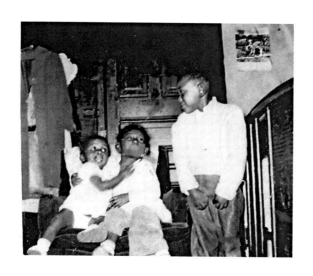

Alvin, Shirley and Isaac

Isaac, Shirley, Alvin and Dorothy Jean Shane

The Inescapable Feeling of Being Alone

Family dynamics have always been one of my greatest challenges, and it started early for me. The real and raw nature of family dynamics and its ability to get next to you, no matter how high the wall you build, leaves you with but one choice and that is to deal with it. The problem for me was that I was too young and ill-equipped to deal with it, so all I could do was suffer through it.

My family dynamics were anything but simple. In July 1953, I became a big brother to a new sibling, John Michael Johnson. Everyone called him "June Bug." I don't know why they called him that; he was born in July and not June. I suspect the name "June Bug" was another way of saying junior. His father was Mr. John Johnson, who lived about two blocks away from us on Lake Park with his common-law wife, Miss Pearl. I don't know when or how my mother met Mr. Johnson. All I know is that having a new baby brother and the accompanying "baby-daddy" drama was more than a notion. Yes, long before the terms "baby-momma drama" or "baby-daddy drama" were ever used, I understood what they meant. The drama with Mr. Johnson was on top of the drama that already existed with Mr. Barlow, the father of my other two siblings.

In some ways, we were fortunate that my father was not in the picture. It could have ended up being a real three-ring circus. But that's not how I really felt. I never knew my father and still to this day have not met him. What I do know is that his name was William Anderson, and that he drove a yellow cab. I was well into my thirties before I was told this by my mom at the insistence of my cousin Johnnie Scott, whom I loved dearly, because she understood my pain. This created a huge void and sense of loss in my life. It caused me to grow up feeling alone and isolated, without a strong sense of connection to my immediate family or extended family. Other than

16

my mother's cousins Rev. Jocephus Curry (from Flint, Michigan), who occasionally came to Chicago for a visit, and J.W. Spencer, who lived on the West Side, I did not know most of my relatives. Although, I had traveled to Alabama with Mrs. Shane and met her family, I never met my grandparents, aunts and uncles, or cousins who lived in the South until I was much older. Later I will talk more about why I never met my grandparents.

I often found myself trying to fit in as an add-on. Most of the time it was very uncomfortable and in the end I was only fooling myself. When Isaac and Shirley spent time with their dad, or we were at the restaurant, where he and my mom worked, I tagged along. When customers or his friends and family would ooh and aah about Isaac and Shirley, they would ask if I was his too. I would turn away to hide my hurt and to spare myself having to see him whisper no. The number of times this happened was too many to count. However, in his defense, he was always pleasant to me and for the most part, whatever they got, I got. Mr. Barlow who was at least 15-20 years older than my mom was proud of his two kids. He had another daughter who was much older than Shirley. You could tell that he was proud of his two youngest kids, in part because most people thought he was too old to have kids their age. I think my mom met him in Detroit, which was the first place she went after leaving DeKalb, Mississippi, where she was born. Isaac, my oldest brother was born in Detroit. By the time Shirley was born, they had moved to Chicago. I don't know when or if they ever lived together, but they did work together a lot.

Other than those painful times when he was asked whether I was his child or when he took Shirley and Isaac to visit his brother John or his sister Mae, I enjoyed being around him. He was a great cook and knew everyone and they all seemed to like him. He would brag that he had fed everybody who lived or worked within a five-mile radius of the restaurant at 37th and

Indiana during one time or another. When they were down on their luck and couldn't go anywhere else (including home) for a meal, he would feed them and most of them never forgot.

The restaurant had a big clock in the front window with a pink film over it to block the intensity of the sun. The cash register was at the front of the restaurant to the left when you entered. Behind it, separating the cashier area from the eat-in counter directly behind it was a white lattice wall you could see through that had vines on it. On the right were small booths that you could sit in and enjoy your meal. At the back of this area on the right was a large juke box that you could pay to play the latest hits. Directly, behind that was a wall that separated the eat-in portion of the restaurant from the back area where the food was stored and prepared. The door leading to the back was on the left portion of the wall behind the counter.

I loved going to the restaurant because it meant I got to eat well and to see more interesting people other than just the ones that lived in my neighborhood. The food at the restaurant was fabulous, the best on the South Side in that area. Customers were quoted saying things like, "that food was so good it would bust your vest". Mr. Barlow cooked most of the meals and made some of the best biscuits and rolls you have ever tasted. My mom helped with the preparation of most of the food, but her specialty was the desserts. Her sweet potato pies, lemon meringue pies, apple pies, peach cobblers, pound cakes, coconut cakes and fried pies were to die for and no customer could leave without having a piece.

Now of course you are probably wondering what fried pies are. To make a fried pie you take pie crust and cut out a circle about 6-8 inches in diameter. Then you place your pie ingredients on half of it before folding the crust in half. Ingredients could include sweet potato pie filling, baked apples processed the same way you make applesauce or peach filling similar to what you would use in a peach cobbler. After folding it in half, take a fork and gently press around the circumference of the crust to seal the ingredients and create a decorative edging. The last step in the process is to drop the pie into boiling hot grease or cooking oil and let it cook until it turns golden brown. If you like, you can sprinkle it with powdered sugar, cinnamon or drizzle icing on top of it.

The other reason I enjoyed going to the restaurant was that I could get paid for helping out, although there was not much I could do. Another added benefit was that we got to go down the street to the photo studio and have our pictures taken by a professional photographer who owned the studio. He was a friend of Mr. Barlow and frequently ate at the restaurant. Many of the nicer pictures taken of us back then that my sister and I have today were taken at that studio. I think the studio was owned by the Gun family that lived in the building next to the orphanage. We sometimes visited the cleaners owned by one of Mr. Barlow's nieces, Seguna (everyone called her Sachy) and her husband, Mr. Cook. They had two children, Peaches and Robert Jr., who were a few years older than Isaac. What I loved about going to the cleaners and visiting Sachy was that she knew I was not one of Mr. Barlow's children, but she treated me, as if I were.

I talked earlier about the "baby-daddy drama" that existed with Mr. Barlow. A lot of the drama was about the way my mother was parenting Isaac and Shirley with most of the concern being about Isaac. He had gotten good grades throughout most of school until he reached fifth grade, when he started becoming rebellious and getting into trouble. He was cutting classes and hanging out with the wrong crowd. Several times when he cut classes and my mother received a call from the school, she would find him at the local pool hall racking balls. She complained to the owner that he was underage and should not be allowed in. This lasted for a little while when the owner was there during the daytime. However, at night and during the weekends, when the owner was not there his employees would let Isaac back in. By now he had begun to perfect the game of pool and fancied himself a young hustler. This caused countless arguments between my mom and his father, who by then were no longer working together. My mother felt she was doing the best she could under the circumstances; being a single mom raising four kids on her own.

The difficulties with Mr. Johnson, my younger brother's father, seemed to start the moment John learned how to talk. John was a chubby little kid that was afraid of everything and who unfortunately, was my responsibility to look after. It meant wherever I went, he went and whatever I did, he had to do. This would have been fine except for the fact that I was a go-getter and the adventuresome type, and he was slow and scared of everything. My friends hated when he had to come along, which was most of the time. A lot of times, I would be left to play alone with him because my friends would take off and leave us behind. The only friend he seemed to have on his own was Regina Jordan, and I could never understand why. However, he did have plenty of enemies.

One enemy was a young lady named Geraldine, who lived in the building next door that was a tomboy. She loved taunting and beating us up, which she did often. Maybe it was because John was always bragging on the things his father and stepmother (Miss Pearl) gave him, which he had a bad habit of doing. One day John and I were playing in the tree house we built in the backyard. Geraldine insisted that we let her come up and play, or else she was going to beat us up. We let her up and not long after that, John said something that made her mad, and she started beating us up. During the scuffle with her, one of us pushed her out of the tree house, and she hurt her arm. She went off screaming, that she was going to get us and tell our mom what we did. Scared out of our minds, we knew we had to do something to stop her from telling. We ran to the building where we lived and hatched a plan to stop her. When we saw her coming through the gangway that separated the two buildings, we threw the rocks at her, so she couldn't come tell our mother. Unbeknownst to me, John had picked up a small brick. When he threw it and hit her on the head, blood started gushing everywhere. We were in big trouble and needless to say we both got a whopping that to this day I will never forget. Geraldine had to get several stitches in her head and had a sprained arm. If there was any upside to the story, it was that she never messed with us again.

As I mentioned, the problems with Mr. Johnson began the moment John started talking. When he visited with his dad and Miss Pearl, he would tell them that he was hungry all the time and never got enough to eat. He complained that we (mostly me) picked on him and never wanted to play with him. We stole his toys from him. We beat him up all the time. The list of complaints was never-ending. Of course when Mr. Johnson confronted my mother with these accusations she would say that John was spoiled and tended to exaggerate. Mr. Johnson was relentless in complaining about how John was being raised. Much of this was instigated by Miss Pearl, who was childless and wanted John to come live with them. After countless fights and altercations with Mr. Johnson, to the point that Isaac and I had to intervene a couple of times, my mother finally acquiesced and John went to live with them when he was five or six. On the weekends John would come and stay with us, or I would go visit him, because ironically he complained all the time that he had no one to play with. Over the years, his father and Mrs. Pearl began to realize what my mother had been trying to tell them about John, but it was too late. He did poorly in school and always blamed everyone else for his shortcomings.

Our neighborhood was filled with families that had moms and dads present in the home and lots of extended family. The lack of extended family was another sore spot for me. Everyone else had grandparents they visited and plenty of cousins who came by to play with them. In fact, in some cases, if you didn't know better, you might think they lived in the neighborhood. I can remember only one time I had a cousin come visit us. It was during one summer and my cousins Patricia, Joseph and Lou Curry from Flint, Michigan came to visit. I was so proud to be able to finally show everyone that I had family too. As memorable as it was for me, I think it was equally memorable for my cousin Joseph. One day he ran out into the street and was almost hit by a car. My mother was horrified and whopped him the same way she would have done one of us. When asked what he was doing, he replied with tears in his eyes, "Aunt Elnora, I was just trying to catch a bird." We still laugh about it when we get together today.

I didn't realize that the constant loneliness, isolation and the sense of not belonging I felt, made me a perfect target for a pedophile. Someone my mother trusted molested me. What troubled me the most was that the person professed to be a Christian and was active in the church. I can't tell you how many times it happened or how frequently it occurred. What I can tell you, in the words of Oprah during an interview with Mo'Nique's brother who raped her, "If it happened one time it was one time too many." The experience left me feeling ashamed, mistrusting and wondering if there was something wrong with me that caused it to happen. It took me a long time to realize that the shame was not on me but on him, and that I did nothing to cause it to happen.

#

The experience of being molested caused me to feel forsaken and question where was God and how He could let this happen to me. I was mad at God and could never see myself ever forgiving the person who molested me. I held on to my anger for years until it turned into cynicism and resentment and ultimately began to affect my relationships with others.

22

One day it came to me that hanging on to these emotions was only hurting me and preventing me from becoming the person I wanted to become. So, I decided to write the names of anyone who had hurt me on a piece of paper and pray until I was no longer consumed with anger or resentment. It took a while but I finally got there and was able to forgive him so that I could move on with my life.

Psalms 22 says "My God, my God, why have You forsaken me? Why are You so far from saving me, so far from the words of my groaning? O my God, I cry out by day, but You do not answer, by night, and am not silent. Yet You are enthroned as the Holy One; You are the praise of Israel. In You our fathers put their trust; they trusted and You delivered them. They cried to You and were saved; in You they trusted and were not disappointed. But I am a worm and not a man, scorned by men and despised by the people. All who see me mock me; they hurl insults, shaking their heads. 'He trusts in the Lord; let the Lord rescue him. Let Him deliver him, since He delights in him.' Yet You brought me out of the womb; You made me trust in You even at my mother's breast. From birth, I was cast upon you; from my mother's womb, You have been my God. Do not be far from me, for trouble is near and there is no one to help.

Mark 11:25 says "When you stand praying, if you hold anything against anyone, forgive him, so that your Father in heaven may forgive you your sins."

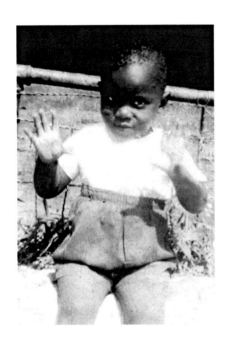

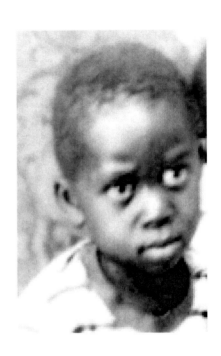

John   **Alvin**

Isaac and Shirley

W. Alvin Jackson's school photos

Kindergarten – 2nd row from top 3rd person from the left

2nd grade – 2nd row from top 3rd person from the left

Struggle May Have Been Her Middle Name but Faith was What She Went By

As far back as I can remember, my mother struggled with the challenges of life almost daily. She struggled to make sure we had enough food, that we could pay the rent, had clean clothes and could afford to buy new ones when we needed them. She worried that we got good grades and stayed out of trouble. Through it all I think she also struggled with her desire to find the right man to have in her life. The unusual part of this for me was that she was never bitter, angry or resentful. It was as if she expected or had grown accustomed to life being a struggle. In spite of it all, she always maintained her faith and tried hard to teach us to do the same.

To really understand my mother, you first need to know a little about her past. I didn't learn much of her past until I was well into my twenties, mostly because she did not talk a lot about it. All I knew is that she was from DeKalb Mississippi. DeKalb is located about 45 miles north of Meridian, Mississippi and 125 miles east of Jackson, Mississippi. Her mother and father were Fannie and Sam Curry. She was the youngest girl and was called Babe. I later found out that she had 13 siblings. There were seven boys: Bill, Percy, Odis, James Arthur (Brutin), William (Bud), Johnnie B. and Floyd. Her six sisters were Beatrice, Lillie, Daisy, Lorraine, Azalee and Maude. Both of her parents came from similar size families. Her father was one of thirteen children. Her mother, whose maiden name was Jack, came from a family of fourteen children.

My grandfather, Sam Curry, was industrious and a progressive thinker well before his time. He owned 350 acres of timberland in Kemper County where DeKalb was located. He lived in a big house and was one of the first Blacks in the area to own a new car. Throughout DeKalb, he was respected by Whites and Blacks for being ambitious and hardworking. He

27

was also a taskmaster when it came to requiring his children to work the land. Many of them resented having to do so and felt that as his children they should not have to work so hard. One of his oldest sons, Percy, didn't mind, because like the others he had been told he would inherit his share of the land upon the passing of my grandfather. Many of his children, tired of having to work the land so hard, moved away despite the promise made to them about inheriting the land. My Uncle Brutin was one of the ones who left and ultimately ended up in Pensacola, Florida. Uncle Bud, who was one of my favorites, married his childhood sweetheart, Aunt Colleen, and they moved to California. He was definitely my favorite uncle because he was funny and made me laugh. He and my mother could have passed for twins they looked so much alike. He was tall, charming and a great storyteller. I could listen to him tell stories about some of the things that happened to them as children all day long and never get bored. I also liked the idea that his first name, William, was the same as mine, although I seldom use my first name other than for legal purposes. In fact, I thought I was named after him until I found out differently. All of my aunts remained in the area. My mother was the only one of the girls to leave.

My grandmother Fannie worked the land alongside my grandfather and their children. She didn't mind hard work because she was use to it. What she did mind was being a second-class citizen in her own home or being disrespected as a woman. Being one of the few successful Black men in the area garnered my grandfather a lot of attention from women in the area. Having one of the largest homes in the area sometimes meant when Blacks visited the area and needed a place to stay, they would come to Mr. Sam. My grandfather would rent out rooms to them, knowing there was no place else they could stay. One of those visitors was a lady named Miss Sophie. She was an educated woman from somewhere in Louisiana. I don't know what transpired between Miss Sophie and my grandfather but my grandmother left and took the kids. They went to stay in a small shack-like house that was on the land. Miss Sophie remained in the house and later she and my grandfather got married. What was not known until much later was that my grandmother and grandfather had never married, which was common back then. In nine states, Mississippi not being one of them, their relationship would have been considered a common-law marriage. They co-habitated, had fourteen children together, held out to the public that they were husband and wife and for the most part, agreed they were married.

The union between my grandfather and Miss Sophie did not last long. She became disenchanted with life in a small town and decided it was time to move on. She hired a lawyer and was granted a divorce that included a financial settlement, which my grandfather refused to pay. To enforce the settlement, her lawyer got the sheriff to trick my grandfather into coming to town, so they could have him locked up. While he was locked up, she hired a logging company to clear-cut a section of the land. The money she received from the timber they cut was her settlement.

Meanwhile my grandmother continued to suffer in silence during all of this. The older kids went out on their own, and the younger ones, including my mother, stayed with my grandmother. Several of the older ones remained in the area. Aunt Lorraine went to work for Dr. Creekmore and his family. Uncle Percy stayed with my grandfather. Azalee was one of the kids that stayed with my grandmother and mother. However, she was becoming rebellious and wanted to hang out at night but my grandmother thought she was not mature enough. Upset with my grandmother for refusing to let her go out, she began putting rat poison in her food, which ultimately caused her death. Her death was tragic and left my mother and her other siblings who had stayed with my grandmother homeless. A few of them, including my mother went back to live with my grandfather whose situation by then had changed. He had remarried and things were different.

The new wife was Miss Barbara, a schoolteacher from Jackson, Mississippi, who moved in as a border and ultimately worked her way up to become his wife. She was very tall, about 6' 2," which made her slightly taller than my grandfather. She was a charmer and a grande dame who needed to be the center of attention. She brought to the relationship a sense of high society. She purchased antiques and made the house feel more like a home. On the surface, she welcomed the children back after the death of their mother. However, she made it very clear that she was my grandfather's wife and in charge, and that they had to abide by her rules in order to stay.

The loss of her mother and having to deal with Miss Barbara was more than my mother could take, so she soon moved out of the house and went to stay with her older sister, Aunt Lorraine. A few years later she decided it was time to leave DeKalb and go north. First stop on her journey north was Detroit where she found a job working as a waitress, in what was called back then the soda fountain/ice cream parlor section of a drugstore owned by Sidney Barthwell. The Barthwells were a prominent family in Detroit that owned a chain of nine drugstores. What's ironic is that in the late '70s when I moved to Detroit I purchased a home in the Boston-Edison Historic District directly across from the Barthwells. I became good friends with their son, Sidney Barthwell Jr. It was in Detroit where my mother met Mr. Barlow and gave birth to her first child, Isaac.

As you can see my mother's life long before she arrived in Chicago had been filled with tragedy, loss and disappointment. While she was no stranger to struggle, she understood the power of prayer, and that faith would see you through. I think that is why one of her favorite songs was the one with the lyrics "There is no secret what God can do. What He has done for others He will do for you." She sang it all the time.

They say that God won't put any more on you than you can bear. It looks like God was truly testing my mother's limits and especially the limits of her faith. She may have stumbled and fallen at times, but she never wavered in her faith and belief that He would see her through it. She believed that if you just keep standing you would make it over. She tried to teach us these lessons and many more through the way she lived her life and the songs and Bible verses she showered us with daily.

In Deuteronomy 6 it says, "Love the Lord Your God. These are the commands, decrees and laws that the Lord your God has directed me to teach you to observe in the land that you are crossing the Jordan to possess. Do this so that you, your children and their children after them may fear the Lord your God as long as you live by keeping all His decrees and commands that I give you. If you do this you will enjoy long life. Hear, O Israel, and be careful to obey so that it may go well with you, and that you may increase greatly in a land flowing with milk and honey, just as the Lord, the God of your fathers, promised you.

Hear, O Israel: The Lord our God, the Lord is one. Love the Lord your God with all your heart and with all your soul and with all your strength. These commandments that I give you today are to be upon your hearts. Impress them on your children. Talk about them when you sit at home and when you walk along the road, when you lie down and when you get up. Tie them as symbols on your hands and bind them on your foreheads. Write them on the door frames of your houses and on your gates."

Sam Curry

Miss Barbara with nieces

Percy Curry with Geneva & Tom

Lorraine Curry

Rev. Dr. Josephus Curry

William (Bud) Curry

Arussell and Tom Curry

Johnnie B. Jack

Arussell and Mary Ruth Curry

Johnnie B., Miss Barbara, Elnora and Irene

We Always Had Church
When We Had Nothing Else

When I say we had church when we had nothing else, I am not just talking in the physical sense but in the spiritual sense as well. For us "church" was more than the building where we worshiped; it was the presence of the Lord in our daily life. Throughout most of my life, I have felt His presence, and it started long before I could explain what I was feeling. It was all those times when my mother seemed at her wits' end because she had more month than she had money. Somehow we were able to stretch the money to cover the month. There were also those times when we were faced with what seemed to be insurmountable challenges and something miraculous would happen to make them disappear.

God's presence manifested itself in our lives in many ways, from the desire to go to church and the reciting of scriptures to the singing of my mother's favorite gospel songs. In retrospect what we lacked in worldly possessions we made up for with spiritual guidance. As early as three or four years of age, I remember being dragged to church. Many of the times we went it was with neighbors who lived in the building. In the beginning Mrs. Dunigan invited us to attend West Point Missionary Baptist Church with her. We started going on a regular basis on our own because West Point was within walking distance and easy for us to get to. Several of our friends attended so we would walk to church with them. West Point was considered back then a large church in contrast to the many storefront churches that existed in Black neighborhoods. It was very traditional; with the prevailing attitude being that children should be seen and not heard. We mostly attended Sunday school and would occasionally join my mother for Sunday Worship Service. The problem with doing that was we had to sit quietly for what seemed like an eternity. In Sunday school, we were taught the typical children's Bible verses and sang children's hymns, like "Jesus loves me, this I know, for the Bible tells me so." One bright spot was Easter Sunday and the Easter play that we all had a part in. I remember being scared to death, but I don't remember the lines I was given to memorize, which I practiced every day until I could deliver my part without forgetting a single word.

I don't know why we switched churches, but we did. We joined a much smaller church that was more of a storefront type. It was led by a woman everybody referred to as Mother Holmes. It was located on 39th Street off of Cottage Grove around the corner from the A&P store and the streetcar barn. It was on the second floor right next door to the Tastee Freeze Store that sold soft-swirl ice cream, shakes, sundaes and banana splits. I didn't mind going to church there on Sunday or during the week for Bible study because if I were lucky and had money I could stop at Tastee Freeze for a treat. Unlike West Point, Mother Holmes's church was more up-close and personal. Everybody knew everybody else in the church and there was no place to hide or play. It was interesting that most of the people, who attended the church, did not live on or close to our block, so I got to make new friends. I was baptized at this church and sang in the junior choir. My mother was more active in this church. She sang in the adult choir, and I think was a Deaconess.

Typical of what happens at many small churches, there was a rift that resulted in splitting the church. Instead of staying with Mother Holmes or going with the Associate Pastor my mother decided to move on. She started going to a new church that one of her friends, Mrs. Rosetta Walker attended, Fellowship Missionary Baptist Church. It was located on 45th and State, and the pastor was Rev. Dr. Clay Evans, formerly of the James Cleveland singers. He was a young and charismatic minister who was known for both his singing and preaching. My mother remained a loyal and faithful member of Fellowship for more than 25 years. She was an usher in the beginning and later became a Deaconess.

I talked about our household being spiritual. My mother would read her Bible and walk through the house reciting Bible verses. You could always tell when times were tough because the tougher they got, the more she read and the more she sang. Although my mother was in the choir, she was no great singer, but she did put her heart into everything she sang. She loved Mahalia Jackson and would go through the house singing many of her songs. Her favorites included "Take My Hand Precious Lord," "Trouble Of The World," "His Eye is on the Sparrow," "How I Got Over," "What A Friend We Have In Jesus" and "Amazing Grace."

The other thing I remember about my mother, which sometimes made me question her spirituality, was her attending the different revivals when they came to town. The two that come to mind were Daddy Grace and Father Devine. There was also a minister from Detroit, who called himself "Prophet Jones." Ironically, he lived in a 54-room house at 75 Arden Park in the same Boston-Edison Historic District in Detroit where I once lived. He would come to town and hold revivals on the lake and my mother and one of her girlfriends would go. They would come back telling stories about how people were healed at the revivals. People who could not see miraculously regained their sight and several in wheelchairs got up and walked. Every revival ended with the customary collection and required a special offering if you wanted to be rubbed with anointing oil or sprinkled with holy water. My mother would also go to Easter Sunrise Services that some of the local ministers would hold on the lake.

#

Watching my mother over the years taught me a lot about faith and prayer. I learned that reading the Bible was the only way to get to know and understand God. Going to church provided an opportunity for fellowship and a chance to praise and worship Him. Prayer can and does change things.

Ephesians 2:1-22 teaches us: "As for you, you were dead in your transgressions and sins, in which you used to live when you followed the ways of this world and of the ruler of the kingdom of the air, the spirit who is now at work in those who are disobedient. All of us also lived among them at one time, gratifying the cravings of our sinful nature and following its desires and thoughts. Like the rest, we were by nature objects of wrath. But because of His great love for us, God, who is rich in mercy, made us alive with Christ even when we were dead in transgressions; it is by grace you have been saved. And God raised us up with Christ and seated us with Him in the heavenly realms in Christ Jesus, in order that in the coming ages He might show the incomparable riches of His grace, expressed in His kindness to us in Christ Jesus. For it is by grace you have been saved, through faith and this not from yourselves, it is the gift of God not by works, so that no one can boast. For we are God's workmanship, created in Christ Jesus to do good works, which God prepared in advance for us to do."

I Thessalonians 5:17–18 says: "Pray without ceasing. In everything give thanks: for this is the will of God in Christ Jesus concerning you."

Fellowship Missionary Baptist Church

Rev. Dr. Clay Evans (Founder & Pastor of Fellowship)

Elnora (on left) in front of the church

Johnnie Scott (my cousin) front row center

CHAPTER 2

THE AWAKENING AND ENLIGHTNING YEARS

Moving on Up

We lived at 3603 Lake Park until 1958, and then we moved to 629 E. 38th Place in the Ida B. Wells projects. I know most people hear the word projects and say, "oh, no." The truth is back then moving into the projects was a step up, especially the low-rise ones like Ida B. Wells compared to the high-rise type. They were built in 1941 as part of the Public Works Administration (PWA) project. It included Madden Park, which had a recreational center with an outdoor swimming pool and playing fields for football and baseball. The units consisted of two-story town houses that shared a common wall with grass in the front and asphalt in the back, and apartments in larger three-story buildings. We lived in a two-story end unit, which meant we also had grass on one side.

Before getting approval to move in, you had to go through a background check and if you or any member of your family had a juvenile or criminal record you would not be approved. We were on a waiting list for more than two years before we got in. We were not the only ones from Lake Park to move into the projects. The Wiley family as well as Plucom and Jerry moved into Stateway Gardens on 35th and State Street.

The families that lived in the other units connected to ours were all very interesting. Next door to us were the Jacksons. Sadie was the mother's name, and she had two sons (James and Noland) and an older daughter (Marlene) who lived with them sporadically. They were all older than us, except for James, who was around my sister Shirley's age. The unit on the other side of them was occupied by the Smith family. It was a family made up mostly of girls (about three or four of them). They lived next door to Tex a kid I played with a lot. The Smith girls were fair-skinned and attractive, for the most part. The mother, Mrs. Smith, drank a lot and always had company and kids running in and out of the house. One of the older

44

girls, Diane, who was very attractive always had suitors coming by. I can remember one night well after midnight; a boyfriend of hers was drunk. He was standing in the back of the house yelling, "Diane do you love me?" Keep in mind the units were all connected and the backyard area was one big row of asphalt. The only separation was the walkway leading up to a raised 2.5' concrete abutment right outside of each back door. There was nothing to buffer the sound. After five minutes of his repeating the question Marlene finally yelled out her back window, "Diane will you please tell that fool you love him, so I can get some damn sleep? I got to go to work in the morning." Embarrassed by Marlene's response and people turning on their backyard lights to see who was keeping everybody up, he disappeared without getting a response from Diane.

At the unit next to the end of our row of town houses was the Wells family. The mother was attractive and always nicely dressed. Whatever she did she must have worked in an office. Mr. Wells always seemed to be in and out. They had three daughters, Diane, Brenda and one who suffered from cerebral palsy, which I knew nothing about at the time. They just seemed to keep her hidden and would occasionally bring her out. Brenda had long pretty hair and wore thick glasses. Diane was medium complexioned and had red hair, an unusual combination.

In the group of row houses to the west of us lived the Martin family, made up of Mrs. Martin and her children, Joseph, Darlene, JoAnn and Shirley. Joseph and I frequently hung out together. A few doors west of them was the Holmes family. The family was made up mostly of boys and they each had a severe case of genu varum (bow-leggedness). It looked as if they had been riding horses all of their lives. Across from them was the Welch family. Everyone in this family was very light-skinned and had unusual colored eyes. By appearance, you would think they would be gentrified, but instead they were just the opposite. Just ask my brother

Barlow about Kenny Welch. He got into one of his many fights in the projects with Kenny Welch, and it was an all-day bring-your-lunch affair. He left that fight with a huge respect for Kenny, and later they became close friends and running buddies.

Two or three doors east of them and diagonally across from us lived the Montgomery family. I can't remember the oldest sister's name but the one about my age was Beatrice. She was brown-skinned, about my complexion, and had big, pretty eyes. I had a crush on her. Her neighbor to the east, located directly across the street from us, was the Knowles family. Their son was Alfred Knowles, who played a musical instrument, which he practiced all the time and was one of my sister's contemporaries.

Everybody I have described thus far lived east, west or to the north of us. To the south of us were other families we played and associated with such as the Williams family. If you walked out of our back yard you would be facing the north side of their house, which faced west. Mr. and Mrs. Williams had two sons, the youngest being Andre, who I played with often. Across from their back yard lived the Reeds. They had two sons and one daughter. Louis Reed was about my age, so he and I hung out. The only problem with Louis was he always went running into the house crying about something that happened. He was probably the least favorite kid in the neighborhood for anyone to play with.

A couple of doors south of the Williams family were the Palmers. Unlike many of the other kids in the neighborhood all the Palmer boys, Lawrence, Alvin and Bucky, went to parochial school. Bucky, who was the oldest, had feminine ways. Alvin was cool and had all the girls chasing him. Lawrence or "Lala" was my friend. He was good-looking like his older brothers except, he had the most severe case of yellow teeth I have ever seen. The next entranceway over was where the Hibler family lived. The mother was Rhoda, her daughter was Carroll and her three sons were Gregory, Adrian and Stephen. Gregory was my best and closest friend. We did everything together. Across the walkway from them was the Larson family. Besides their parents there were Jamie, Margo and Karen. My mother would often use Margo to baby sit my younger brother Tyrone, the latest edition to our family, when one of us was not available.

October 19, 1959 our family grew by one with the addition of our new baby brother Tyrone Marvin Jackson. His father was Bill Dunigan, who, after we moved to the projects, would frequently stop by to visit. When he came to visit everybody in the neighborhood knew he was there. He drove a 1959 tan convertible Cadillac that everybody on the block would come running to see. 1959 marked the beginning of Cadillac's shift in design from the beefier more hefty-looking vehicles to the long and sleek look with the big tail fins. Needless to say Tyrone was an unexpected surprise for all of us and like everything else in our lives we did what we had to do. The only difference in having Tyrone as a baby brother versus John was that I was nine years old when he was born and was not expected to shoulder responsibility for him by myself. He was the shared responsibility of Shirley and me, with her assuming most of the responsibility. The good thing is that she didn't mind taking care of him because Mr. Dunigan would always give her extra money for babysitting him.

There is one story that I have to tell about the three of us. One day my mother dropped us off at Big Hazel's house. I am assuming she had to work that day. Tyrone was still very young and no more than a year and a half old. Big Hazel had made a huge pot of gumbo and offered it to Shirley and me. I had never eaten gumbo before and didn't really enjoy it. After eating the first bowl Big Hazel offered us a second bowl. Now we had been taught that it was not polite to say no when someone was being kind and offering you food. The problem was she thought we liked the gumbo because we ate it so fast. We ate it fast because we didn't like the taste and just wanted to be done with it. When she offered us more she said, "I know it's good and you kids don't have to be shy." Even though we kept insisting that we had had enough she brought us another bowl. Worried and concerned about offending her, we were left with no choice but to start feeding it to Tyrone, who did not mind. When we got home that evening Tyrone had one of the worst cases of diarrhea ever. It was non-stop and of course we had to change him. My mother kept asking what we had fed him, and we finally had to confess that it was the gumbo. As an adult he hated gumbo; the mere smell of it would make him sick.

Living in the projects was enjoyable most of the time. We got to plant flowers with our mom and have barbecues in the backyard. When one of my mother's nephews, Jessie Murray (we called him Junior) from Flint, Michigan would come to town we would have a huge barbecue. He loved to barbecue and made some of the best ribs. My mother would bake a pound cake and make homemade ice cream. I would take the portable record player to the back yard, and the party would get started. All of my friends and the neighbors would stop by and Junior would feed them. Everybody in the neighborhood loved Junior and would ask me when he was coming back.

I had a lot of friends in the neighborhood. We were mischievous but it never resulted in anything really bad happening. When school started, during the weekdays after school we would walk literally two miles to go to the Elliot Donnelley Youth Center located on 40th and Michigan Avenue. We went there two-to-three times a week to play games and swim. I had learned how to swim at Madden Park one summer and now wanted to swim all the time. I was like a fish. While walking to the youth center, we would smoke cigarettes and dare each other to go into the Certified

Grocery store near South Park and steal candy and cookies. We got caught one time and gave back what we stole. We promised never to come back into the store.

On the weekends, it was all about hustling to make money to spend during the week. At first I would go to the Dell Farmer grocery store on 37th and Cottage Grove and then to the A&P on 39th after it opened, to hustle groceries. I would take my wagon or a baby buggy there early Saturday morning and wait outside the exit door and offer to carry customers' groceries home for tips. Sometimes I would get there early and find they needed a bagger because someone had not shown up. I would do that for a while until the missing or late employee would arrive. Normally, I would make enough during the weekend to have spending money for the week.

My stay in Ida B. Wells was great until one day in 1961 when my mother received a letter from the Chicago Housing Authority saying we had to move because my brother Barlow had been caught with his friends breaking into the Madden Park Recreational Center to steal equipment. I was devastated and could not believe this was happening to us. I cried for days and kept asking my mother why we had to move. Why couldn't we just make *him* move? He was fifteen and was staying out late most of the time. It seemed so unfair to me that we were going to have to move for something stupid he did.

We moved to 4423 South Vincennes to an apartment on the fourth floor, and I hated living in this building. It was a big old raggedy building in a neighborhood I had never been to before. I was mad at everyone, mostly my mother and stupid brother. It also meant going to a new school, Forrestville Elementary School. In the winter, we would often be without heat for days. This never happened in any of the other places we had lived.

49

One time it happened and I forgot to move my goldfish (Herkimer) into the dining room and kitchen area. We would camp out in there to be near the heat coming from the stove in the kitchen. The heat coming from the stove was the only heat we had in the apartment. One day when I went back up front to look for something in my room Herkimer was frozen solid.

We stayed in that building for about a year or so and then we moved to 425 E. 42nd Street into a two-family building owned by Mr. Mack. We lived on the second floor in a small apartment. It was clean and we had heat. I knew we were not going to stay there long because it was too small and Mr. Mack, a retired mailman who lived on the first floor, was way too nosy. The only good thing that happened while living there was that I transitioned into a new hustle. I became a newspaper boy, delivering the *Chicago Tribune*, one of the morning newspapers. I would have to get up at 4:30 a.m. so that I could be at the paper stand by 5:15 to pick up my newspapers. I had to complete my route in time to get back home, shower and get dressed so that I could be in school by 8:30.

A year and a half later we moved to 503 E. 44th Street, when I was in the eighth grade. It was a nice apartment in a very large three-story building with 28 units that was well maintained all the time. It was owned by Sol Reisner, who owned several other large buildings in the neighborhood as well as the local hardware store on 43rd Street. For me this was like moving into the courtway building on Lake Park. As a family we remained in that apartment for more than twenty years until I moved my mother to Detroit to live with me in 1983. However, from the time we moved from Lake Park until then it seemed we moved every couple of years.

#

It's clear to me during periods of my life that change, no matter how uncomfortable it might be, was going to be a constant part of my life. I was

50

being prepared for the many changes to come in my life. It taught me that no matter how bad things may seem in the moment, they have a way of working themselves out. I also learned that when He closes one door He is more than likely preparing you for something even better. I have learned from my many experiences that in the midst of a storm you just have to still yourself and wait for that quiet voice to guide you.

Proverbs 3: 5-6 tells us: "Trust in the Lord with all your heart and lean not on your own understanding; in all your ways acknowledge Him, and He will direct your path."

The Serenity Prayer, written by Reinhold Niebuhr, says: "God grant me the serenity to accept the things I cannot change; courage to change the things I can; and wisdom to know the difference. Living one day at a time; enjoying one moment at a time; accepting hardships as the pathway to peace; Taking, as He did, this sinful world as it is, not as I would have it; Trusting that He will make all things right if I surrender to His will; That I may be reasonably happy in this life and supremely happy with Him forever in the next."

Ida B. Wells Housing Projects

Row houses in Ida B. Wells

Shirley next to row house where we lived

Trouble Seemed to Follow Him
Wherever He Went

My brother Isaac Barlow always seemed to walk around under a dark cloud filled with trouble. The problem is, it didn't have to be that way. When he was young he did extremely well in school. Everybody thought he had great potential, and they were right. He could have been a top salesman in any organization, a top corporate or criminal attorney or a very successful entrepreneur. Instead very early on he decided to pursue a life of crime. I have always wondered why he made that choice and did not pursue his purpose in life. It was as if he were doing it to act out his anger and frustration with his father and our mother. I don't know what they did or didn't do that made him so upset, but whatever it was; it set him on a path of destruction. This is one of those times when I am left with more questions than answers. Was it because he felt they didn't love or understand him? Perhaps he was angry that his family structure was not like everybody else's? Maybe he didn't feel a sense of acceptance or connection with his father. Could it have been he was embarrassed by our circumstances and let that develop into a chip on his shoulder, and he was out to prove something? I don't know the answer to any of these questions because our relationship was never close enough for me to ask. Besides he was my "big brother" and someone who I should be looking up to and not questioning.

Here is what I do know and that is, he always seemed angry, was very secretive, and he was a natural-born hustler. I mentioned earlier that he was hanging out in the poolrooms and fancied himself a minor pool shark instead of going to school. Eventually, his ditching school caught up with him, and he was kicked out of Doolittle Elementary School in seventh grade. As a minor he was required to attend school, so he was sent to

Flavel Moseley Public School. Everybody called the school Moseley and knew it was a school for bad boys. It was originally located at 2348 South Michigan and in 1959 moved to 5700 South Lafayette Avenue. He entered the school when it was on South Michigan and graduated from South Lafayette. The school was run by a man referred to as Colonel Smith, whom everybody called the Colonel.

The Colonel was known for being strict and not taking any stuff. If you got out of line, he would administer strong corporal punishment. His job, plain and simple, was to turn bad kids into good kids. While discipline was important the Colonel tried to help them understand and deal with the things that were causing them to act out. Every student was required to participate in an extracurricular activity, and my brother chose to play the drums in the marching band. They were also required to memorize poems. We spent hours and weeks helping Barlow memorize "Casey at the Bat," a poem writing by Ernest L. Thayer that appeared in the 1888 issue of *The Examiner*. The poem was to teach that life can be challenging and unpredictable; that no matter what it hands you, step up to the plate and take a clean swing at it regardless of the outcome.

For the first time, it seemed as if maybe Barlow was turning a corner and getting his life back on the right track. I think the Colonel felt that way too and when he graduated in January 1960 had him recite the poem "Invictus" by William Ernest Henley.

Invictus

Out of the night that covers me,
Black as the Pit from pole to pole,
I thank whatever gods may be
For my unconquerable soul.

In the fell clutch of circumstance
I have not winced nor cried aloud.
Under the bludgeonings of chance
My head is bloody, but unbowed.

Beyond this place of wrath and tears
Looms but the Horror of the shade,
And yet the menace of the years
Finds, and shall find, me unafraid.

It matters not how strait the gate,
How charged with punishments the scroll.
I am the master of my fate:
I am the captain of my soul.

William Ernest Henley

After graduating from Moseley Barlow entered Wendell Phillips High School on 39th and Prairie. Unfortunately, as much as we had hoped, he still had not changed. He used to hang out with several of the fellows in the neighborhood, including Kenny Welch and Little Marvin. Now that he and Kenny had become friends his new nemesis was a guy named Herschel Lee. They would get into a fight almost daily, and he would chase my brother home. One day my mother told him she was tired of him running in the house hiding from Herschel Lee. She made it clear to him that he was going to have to fight him or fight her. The choice was his. The next time it happened, he decided to fight, and they fought all the way home and much to my brother's surprise, he held his own. The stories were running wild in the projects about the fight and how Barlow hit Herschel Lee in the head with a brick and then wrestled him to the ground, throwing punch after punch and would not let him up. This only added to his growing reputation of being "bad" and not someone you messed with. The problem for me was that everybody expected me, who they now referred to as "little Barlow," to go for bad as well. This caused me to experience more than my fair share of fights trying to live up to a reputation I had no interest in upholding.

I don't want to paint the picture that the only thing he did was get in trouble. Like the rest of us, he worked. In our house, there was an unwritten rule that Elnora (my mother) only provided the basics: food, essential clothing and shelter. Once you reached a certain age (nine or ten) you were expected to earn your own spending money and purchase whatever additional clothing you wanted or felt you needed outside of the essentials she provided. Barlow had a paper route working for a guy everyone called "Cheap Charlie," delivering the *Sun Times,* and he also shined shoes on the weekend. Cheap Charlie and Ed, the guy he shined shoes for, loved him because he did a great job and the customers loved him. He would come home with tons of loose change he received as tips from his customers. He earned enough money to keep himself well dressed all the time and added being sharp to his "rep" (reputation).

In his sophomore and junior years at Wendell Phillips, he began making friends and hanging out with guys who didn't live in the Ida B. Wells projects with us. There were three guys he became friends with, Bill Adkins, James (Hut) Hudson and Little Joe. Bill Adkins went to DuSable High School and was a pretty good athlete. Hut lived in Wentworth Gardens, a different project, was fast-talking and a bit of a con man. Little Joe was the "coolest" of the four and definitely a ladies' man. They hung out together and worked on schemes to get money. It didn't matter to them whether they were legal or not. This became Barlow's gateway to take his pool hustling to a new level and move into becoming a street hustler.

57

#

There is a turning point in most of our lives where we have to decide whether to pursue the "evil forces" leading us in one direction or hearken to the voice of God inside of us, leading us toward our purpose. The problem is that oftentimes following the evil forces leads to immediate gratification and the potential for greater pleasure or gain. Pursuing one's purpose and destiny is normally fraught with sacrifice and uncertainty. It is a tough choice for most of us, but it comes down to whether you believe in God.

According to Romans 8: 28: for those of us who do believe in God, we know that "God causes everything to work together for the good of those who love God and are called according to his purpose for them."

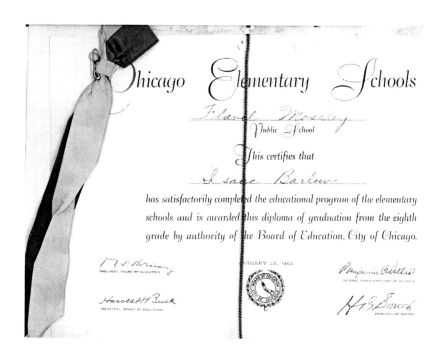

Isaac's eight grade diploma

Wendell Phillips High School

Discovering How to Soar

For the most part, school through fourth grade was a non-event: I wasn't a particularly good student nor was I a bad one. I was an average student getting by, which is how I saw myself. It wasn't until fifth grade that I realized that I had potential. Prior to this, my teachers may have realized it, but it had not sunk in with me. In fifth grade, I attended Oakland Elementary School located on 40th between Langley and Cottage Grove, not far from where we lived in the projects. My fifth grade teacher for part of the school year was the principal of the school, Mrs. O'Connor. She somehow sparked something in me that made me begin to think that if I applied myself, I could get better grades. It was an idea I was beginning to like.

By the time I arrived at Forrestville Elementary school to begin 6th grade, after we moved to 44th and Vincennes, things had changed, and I was now considered a good student. I was placed in classes with other students who were classified as smart, which meant I was smart. My teacher was Mrs. Cross, a tall redheaded teacher who was fairly even-tempered until you made her mad. By now I was beginning to have a sense of my academic strengths. I did exceptionally well in math, spelling and writing. Science was definitely not my forte, and I got by in history and language art. I was a C+/B+ student with strong potential to be an A student.

I was new to the area and the school and trying to feel my way around, so I was quiet most of the time. However, it was clear which kids were really smart, which were the class clowns and which ones were just trying to get by. The smartest one in the class was a girl name Carolyn Hull. She was a straight-A student. In terms of the boys in the class, there was a kid name Edward Kirk, who seemed to be fairly smart. The problem was that he stuttered badly and no one could understand what he was

60

saying. What's funny is that if you asked others in the class who was the smartest boy, they would probably say me. The nicest dressers in the class were unquestionably Sam Lemon and Derrick Agins. I didn't dress badly but I was not at their level of dressing.

In addition to Mrs. Cross, there were other teachers who seemed to take an interest in their students and showed they cared. There was Mrs. Harman, a tall lanky woman who loved to wear dangling jewelry. She was a fun-loving and carefree teacher, but she absolutely would not tolerate misbehaving. If you did, she would grab you by the meat of your arm and pinch and twist it so hard you wanted to cry. I saw her do this to one of her students when we were in the hallway during a fire drill. It did not matter whether you were in her class or not. If you got out of line, and she was around, she'd come charging at you.

The other teacher who really seemed to care was Mrs. Thompson, the librarian. She was a petite, soft-spoken woman, but she meant business. She would give you the evil eye, which was her way of warning you to stop what you were doing. If you didn't stop, she made you put your hand out so she could smack it with a triangular shaped ruler she kept in her desk.

Entering seventh grade, which meant we transferred to Forrestville Upper Grade Center, was tantamount to kids of today going to a middle school. Instead of remaining in the same class all day we rotated classes and had lockers for storing our books and coats. My seventh grade homeroom teacher was Mr. Bowie, a paddle-toting Alpha. I had him for language arts as well. If you got out of line he would have what he called a "paddle party with Mr. Do Right." For the boys he would give you the choice of walking the line and letting the other boys paddle you or having him give you three whacks across the behind. Of course everybody chose having

61

the other boys do it because they didn't hit as hard, plus they would cut you some slack. He, on the other hand, would grab your belt in the back and twist it so your pants would tighten up on your behind and start whaling. If the girls got out of line, he would use the small triangular ruler on their hands like the one Mrs. Thompson used, instead of the paddle.

The most memorable thing that happened while at Forrestville Upper Grade Center was the death of President John F. Kennedy. I distinctly remember the day it happened in November 1963. We had just returned from lunch and were sitting in our 5th period class. Someone from the school office came in and whispered something to our teacher who immediately proceeded to turn on the radio in our classroom. We heard the radio announcer say that President Kennedy had been shot and later said he was dead. We sat there in shock not knowing what to do or say. We all felt a sense of tremendous loss that day.

Shortly after graduating from Forrestville Upper Grade Center, expecting to attend DuSable High School in the fall, we were notified there was a change of plans. DuSable, which was the feeder high school for kids that lived in my neighborhood, was too crowded to handle all the incoming freshmen. The school district decided to have the students from Forrestville Upper Grade Center remain there for the ninth grade as an interim solution and bring in ninth grade teachers. A new plan was initiated to accelerate finishing building Carter G. Woodson Elementary School, which would replace Forrestville Elementary School. The facility used for Forrestville Elementary could then be used for the Upper Grade Center. The Upper Grade Center would be turned into a four-year high school until a new one could be built four years later.

It was disappointing beginning my freshman year of high school in the same building, but they made a lot of changes to make it feel more like a high school. The most notable and obvious was the new administration and teachers. The new school principal on an interim basis was Mrs. Daniels, formerly the upper grade center counselor. The assistant principal was Mr. Anderson Thompson, the husband of the Forrestville Elementary School librarian.

High school was a lot different because in addition to your regular class work you were expected to be involved in other school activities. This was especially true for the kids I had classes with which were mostly advance and honor classes. We were expected to be school leaders and go to college. I hadn't thought much about going to college but now everything we did was centered on preparing for college. Going to college became the central theme behind everything we did and the person leading the charge was the assistant principal, Anderson Thompson. He seemed to be the man with the plan. One of the first things that he did was to create a tutoring program with Wheaton College. Every Wednesday right after school we would be bused 30 miles from the South Side to Wheaton, Illinois. There we would be tutored in whatever subject we were struggling with.

Mr. Thompson who at some point became Dr. Thompson in concert with the new principal, Barbara Sizemore embarked on a program to teach us Black history and more about our heritage. He developed various programs to do that including creating a group called "The Magnificent 7." Symbolic of the spirit of the "Seven Samurai," Dr. Thompson assembled seven male students portraying seven famous Black leaders past and present with the mission of broadening the student body's awareness of the contributions, they made to society. I was selected to play Marcus Aurelius Garvey. Robert Hayes was chosen to be Booker T. Washington. Dewitt Minyard was W.E.B. Dubois. Robert Davenport portrayed the colorful Adam Clayton Powell. Leroy Ousley played Carter G.

Woodson. James Brown was the embodiment of Malcolm X. Derrick Agins transformed himself into Dr. Martin Luther King Jr. Lesly Flanagan invoked Stokely Carmichael. Charles Welch was H. Rap Brown. John Douglas re-enacted his namesake Frederick Douglas. In case you were counting, yes there were more than seven of us. We started with seven and added characters along the way making us the Magnificent 7 + 1 or the Magnificent 7 + 2.

Each one of us had to craft a three-to-five-minute speech representing the character we were portraying. In some cases, we could use the actual speeches given by the character we represented. This was easy for several of the guys in the group because of the wealth of information and speeches available on their characters. I understand now why he created the group. First, it gave us a reason to do research on Black leaders. Second, it made it easier for the student body to learn about these leaders versus giving them an assignment to read about them. Lastly, it helped prepare us for leadership roles.

Once we completed our research and prepared our speeches, Dr. Thompson assembled the entire student body to hear our presentations. It went exceptionally well and Dr. Thompson got the bright idea that we should take the show on the road, and that is exactly what we did. He arranged for us to make presentations to different groups around the city and nearby communities surrounding Chicago. We even took it on the road to other cities both in and outside of the state. During the process, we developed our confidence and became strong public speakers. Along the way, we bonded and became best friends.

While Dr. Thompson was working with us, he enlisted the aid of another teacher, Beverly Ball, to form a similar group with the girls called "I Too Sing America." Miss Ball had just started teaching and was excited to

64

take on the assignment. Like the young men, the girls assumed the identify of famous Black women such as Sojourner Truth, Harriett Tubman, Ida B. Wells, Madam C. J. Walker, Rosa Parks and Dorothy Height. The girls did an excellent job of representing their characters, but for some reason it did not last as long as the Magnificent 7. Miss. Ball put as much energy into it as did Dr. Thompson; the difference is it became a life line for us.

#

This period of my life was all about being prepared and trained. On the surface it appears, there was not a lot going own spiritually. I would disagree in that I believe positive growth is spiritually based. God put me in a position to receive the right amount of training, nurturing and caring needed to build a strong foundation for the journey that lay ahead. I have weathered many of life's storms because of the undergirding I received during this time of my life.

Proverbs 22:6 says, "Train a child in the way he should go, and when he is old he will not turn from it."

W. Alvin Jackson – Forrestville Upper Grade Center

6th grade – center row 2nd from right

8th grade graduation – 2nd row far right

Forrestville High School

The Magnificent 7

Dr. Anderson Thompson

Friendship, Respect and Trust

Attending Forrestville Upper Grade Center provided me with the opportunity to begin making friends, slowly but surely. By the time I got to high school and became a member of the Magnificent 7, I had more friends than I knew what to do with. My closest friends ended up being the other guys in the Magnificent 7.

I met Derrick Agins first, as he was in my sixth-grade class, but I became friends with Dewitt Minyard first. Dewitt lived in a large building diagonally across from us on the northwest corner of 44th and Vincennes. By then we were living at 503 E. 44th Street. Dewitt was what the girls called "fine" or good looking. He was about 5'10", light complexioned with dimples and short wavy hair. He had no problems getting the girls. He lived with his mother and father (Amanda and Dewitt senior) along with his sister Mamie, who was older, his big brother Eural and younger brother Jerrold. Mr. Minyard worked at the steel mill. Dewitt prided himself on being cool, which today might be misconstrued as being slightly aloof. He knew he didn't have to chase the girls because they would come to him. All he had to do was pick and choose. He has maintained that same demeanor throughout most the years I have known him and still does today. We became friends because I lived across from him, was smart and dressed fairly well.

When Derrick was in my sixth-grade class, I did not like him at all and could have never envisioned us becoming friends. He was Sam Lemon's sidekick. They both wore expensive (often tailor-made) clothes and seemed to look down on everyone else. I discovered through hanging out with him as one of the members of the Magnificent 7, that he was slightly shy and overall a nice guy. Sam was the one who was snobbish. Derrick was large for his age, about 6'1" and big boned like his father James Agins. Everybody called his dad "Big Jim," who was truly a hard drinking hell raiser. He was big in stature around 6'3' and at least 275 pounds. His mother Bernice Agins, on the other hand, was a small well-built woman with a heart of gold. Derrick had three siblings: Richard his older brother, Betsy his big sister and Cynthia his younger sister. Mr. Agins worked for the Sherwin Williams Paint Company and was known to come home drunker than "Cooter Brown" on Friday and stay that way most of the weekend. As big as he was, Derrick was a gentle soul with child-like qualities stuck in a grown-up body. Throughout high school, he dated Marion Brunson, who was built like a brick you know what. It was clear that she was the dominant one in that relationship. Derrick lived on 43rd and Forrestville (a block from where I lived). At lunchtime, he and I would walk home from school together and after a while go home to my house or his for lunch. When my mother got a full time job working as a cook at a school near the Ida B. Wells projects, I went home with Derrick every day for lunch and his mother never minded. On the weekends, he would always drop by to see what my mother was cooking. If it were something he preferred over what his mom was cooking, he would stay and eat. In fact, there were times when I would come home and find him sitting there with my mom eating. My mom liked Derrick and called him "Hungry Jack."

Lesly Flanagan became my friend through Dewitt. Initially, I did not care for him and thought he was a short arrogant conceited bastard. He always walked around comparing what he was wearing to what you had on. He was extremely materialistic and based on that you would have thought he was from a middle class family with money. He also had what I call an "excess driven personality" meaning everything he did was excessive. He had an insatiable appetite for everything from money and drugs to sex. In

70

the beginning, I just tolerated him and would only be around him if Dewitt were there. He was in several of my classes in high school and was a member of the Magnificent 7. I think I began to warm up to him after I went to his home and met his mother, grandmother and sister. He lived in a building on 44th and Calumet owned by his mother's aunt. When you walked into their apartment instead of entering the living room, you walked into his grandmother's bedroom. The next room was the bedroom where he and his sister Eloise slept. From there you entered his parent's bedroom and after that were the bathroom and a small kitchen. They did not have a living room, dining room or much closet space. It was clear to me after seeing where he lived that he was very insecure and did the things he did almost as a preemptive strike. He also seemed to suffer from a Napoleon complex. His mother, Mrs. Lucy Flanagan, worked for a florist shop owned by his great aunt on 43rd Street, and his father George worked at a liquor store owned by Lamar (his great aunt's son).

Bob Hayes, I liked the moment, I met him. He was down to earth and some would say a bit country. There was nothing pretentious or phony about him. He lived on 42nd and Champlain with his mother and father and younger brother, Willis. Bob was tall and thin about 6'3" and seemed to enjoy life. He was actively involved in the church he attended with his parents and would sometimes invite me to come along. I hung out with him a lot because he was the easiest to relate to and someone I could have serious conversations with. He was truly a confidant for me. We were friends for a long time until his tragic death in 2002. He died from a drug overdose, but I think it was because he lost his way. One of my biggest regrets is that after college and in the ensuing years, I did not keep in contact with him. I often wonder whether being a closer friend might have made a difference. When he died, I attended his funeral, and as I sat there watching Marie (his estranged wife) and their kids, I felt a great loss not just for me but for his kids as well. It prompted me to write a poem, which I had made into a plaque and gave to each of his children signed with his name as the author.

THE CHOICE IS YOURS

Choose hanging in with school
So you won't end up hanging out with fools.
Choose to get high on life
So you won't end up low on drugs.
Choose to jump the hurdles along the road to success
So you don't end up in the potholes down the road to failure.
Choose to see yourself and your children as the focus of your love
And not as the product of your love.
Remember, The choice is yours and ...
If you choose giving, you'll never have to worry about receiving.
If you choose helping, you will never have to worry about being helped
If you choose loving, you will never have to worry about being loved.
Finally, if you choose God, you'll never have to worry again.

—Robert L. Hayes (W. A. J.)

Leroy Ousley lived the farthest from us on 40th and Drexel. He was about the same complexion as Dewitt and had the same grade of hair. Like Dewitt, he was cool and had no problems attracting the ladies. He was much shorter than Dewitt, about 5'7" or 5'8," but he was very muscular. He lifted weights with a couple of his friends, Willie Sanford and Randolph Hardy. I am not sure whether it was Lesly or Bob that introduced him to the group. I was a little reluctant about him because he seemed a little too self-indulgent. It took me a long time to finally get to know him and warm up to him. He was always talking about being strong and how much he could lift and bench press. As a skinny little kid, I didn't want to hear anything about being strong and had no intentions of taking up weight lifting, which he frequently suggested I should do. I later discovered that he was at one time a skinny little kid like me, who I am sure, was picked on by the bigger kids, until he started lifting weights. Over time, he became more accepting of me for who I was and when that happened, we stared to become friends.

Every group has to have a jock and for us, it was John Douglas. John was very athletic and excelled in basketball. He was about 5'6" or 5'7" and played guard on the school's basketball team. His younger brother Frederick played on the football team. He came from a large family with six or seven kids, and he was the oldest. They lived with their mom and dad on 44th and Indiana. His dad was quite a bit older than his mom and there was never a dull moment in their house. John's athleticism made him very confident and self-absorbed on the court; off the court, he struggled a bit academically even though he was bright. I think it was just a matter of more emphasis being placed on sports than academics. John was hotly pursued by the ladies but managed to limit his affections to one girlfriend, Patsy Rogers through most of high school. John and I were friends, and it didn't matter one iota to him that I was not athletic. I think I appealed more to his academic side and did not see him as just another dumb jock.

Meeting girls and dating was not easy for me. I was more of a skinny "well-dressed" nerd than anything else. I could not trade on my looks or athletic abilities; instead, I had to rely on being a nice guy, who was smart with a future ahead of me and being well dressed. Back then your style of dress was Ivy League, Gouster or Continental. Ivy Leaguers wore button-down oxford shirts; the most popular being Brooks Brother. For trousers, they wore un-pleated pants (many of which were khaki) with a small cuff and a buckle on the back with buck skinned shoes or leather penny loafers. It was always topped off with a wool high-boy or eight piece cap. Gousters wore big pleated baggy pants, knit shirts, a Fedora hat and Johnson & Murphy shoes. Most Gousters were gang-bangers. Continental was a cross between a Gouster and an Ivy Leaguer. Derrick Agins was definitely Continental. He wore expensive Italian knit sweaters, tailor-made pants (no pleats and cuffs) that was oftentimes personalized with his initials embroidered on the front waistband. They wore alligator or lizard shoes and knit caps. They dressed like the actor Dick van Dyke but a little more soulful. I was an Ivy Leaguer from top to bottom and had more Brooks Brothers shirts than anyone else. Your shirts had to be heavily starched to have the right look. The reason I had more than anyone else, was because I was so skinny that I could purchase them from the boys department for ten dollars cheaper. Since I had a newspaper route and was the branch captain I could afford to buy a lot of clothes.

I must digress at this point to tell you the story, of how I became branch captain. I worked for a man name George Washington. He had a reputation for being shady. He had this huge black Great Dane called Sinbad that he kept locked in the back. He would tell everyone not to go in the back because the dog was vicious and would attack. One day I was in the branch waiting for one of the other paperboys to finish his route. Mr. Washington had to run out to get cigarettes and forgot to lock the door to the back where he kept Sinbad. I didn't know the door was unlocked and the dog pushed the door open and came galloping toward me. I just knew I was a goner and instead of him attacking me, he licked me to death. When Mr. Washington came back and saw me sitting on the floor playing with Sinbad, he said don't tell anyone, it will just be our little secret.

At the end of every week on a Sunday you got paid for delivering the newspapers. How much you got paid depended on the number of papers you delivered and the value of your receipt book. The receipt book had one page for each customer, showing how much they owed, and you needed to collect. Mr. Washington used a sliding scale method to determine how much you were paid for each paper delivered. The maximum you would be paid was 15 cents per paper depending on what percent of your book you collected. If you had a route with 200 customers and collected 95 percent or more of your book you would receive 15 cents per paper and get paid $30.00. Every time I tried to figure out how much I should be paid; it never seemed to jive with how much per paper he said I should be paid. Believe it or not he used a slide ruler to figure out how much per paper you should be paid. Frustrated with the sense I had that I was being cheated; I enlisted the help of my math teacher to teach me how to use a slide ruler. In fact, she gave me one to practice with that she later let me keep. Armed with my new ability, the next Sunday when it was time to settle up, I whipped out my slide ruler after he had calculated how much I should be paid per paper. I looked at him and said, "Let's see what my slide ruler has to say about that" and just as I suspected, he had been cheating me. It wasn't by a lot but for me every penny counted. The following week when I came in he said since you are so smart, I am going to make your branch captain. I got a raise and kept my mouth shut about what he was doing. I probably should have told the other guys but most of them didn't like me anyway.

Let's get back to the matters of the heart. I dated several girls in high school and one of them was a young lady named Rosemary Ricks. She lived across the street from Lesly on 44th and Calumet. In fact, it was Lesly, who introduced me to her. She was two years behind me in school and lived with her mom and dad. She had two sisters and one brother. Her

75

brother Junior who was older and her younger sister Candy lived at home. Her older sister Ada was married and had a family that lived elsewhere. Rosemary was a nice young lady who looked up to me and trusted me. I was a junior in high school going into my senior year, and she was a rising sophomore when she got pregnant. I didn't know what to do and like a lot of young men, I denied it was mine. I buried my head in the sand and kept doing what I had been doing.

I want to stop here and offer my heartfelt apology to her for not being matured enough to do what was right. Besides acknowledging that I got her pregnant and was the father of her child, I want to take this opportunity to apologize to her for violating her trust and somehow thinking my potential was more important than hers. I didn't realize at the time that my behavior (engaging her sexually) was selfish, reckless and showed no regard for how it could potentially impact her life. In spite of it all, she showed a level of strength far greater than any, I have had to. She went on with her life as a young mother with the help of her family. She graduated from high school and went on to college graduating with a degree in nursing. Today she has a Ph.D. and is an Assistant Professor of Nursing at a local college in Chicago.

#

While respect and trust are essential for friendship and other personal relationships, the most important part of any relationship is being there. This life's lesson has been one of the more painful I have had to learn.

The Bible speaks to friendship in Ecclesiastes 4: 9-12. It says, "Two are better than one; because they have a good reward for their labor. For if they fall, the one will lift up his fellow, but woe to him that is alone when he falleth for he hath not another to keep him up. Again, if two lie together, then they have heat; but how can one be warm alone. And if one prevails against him, two shall withstand him; and a threefold cord is not quickly broken."

Derrick Agins

Dewitt Minyard

Lesly Flanagan

Leroy Ousley

Robert Hayes

John Douglas

Rosemary Ricks and Richard Anthony Ricks-Jackson

The People and Programs that Shaped My Life

The fall of 1965, the beginning of my sophomore year, was a major turning point in my life. I started participating in a program called "Education for Life." We met every Tuesday after school at the Firman House located on 47th and Federal, next door to the Robert Taylor Homes (another group of high-rise projects like Stateway Garden). The director of the program was Dr. Thaddeus Kostrubala. The purpose of the program was to expose kids with high potential, from disadvantaged backgrounds, to a variety of professionals as a means of inspiring them. Every week we would have a different guest speaker come to share with us their background and how they got to where they are now.

One week a speaker canceled at the last minute and Dr. Kostrubala decided to have his wife Ingrid, who was from Sweden, come and talk to the group. Instead of talking with us about her profession, she talked about Sweden and what a great place it was. She described Sweden in a fairy-tale like manner, as a place that was so clean that you could, figuratively speaking, eat off the ground. One of the students, Lesley Flanagan, whose only real point of reference was the South Side of Chicago, thought she was over exaggerating. He said to her in a challenging manner; "lady you must think we are stupid, there is no place like that anywhere." Frustrated and a bit taken aback by his comment, she replied, "I'll just have to show you." When she got home that evening, she shared her experience with her husband, Dr. Kostrubala, and he was disturbed that she had broken one of his cardinal rules —never make promises to kids (especially poor ones) that you can't keep. Everyone else that worked at the Firman House knew of this rule. She of course was unaware of the rule and didn't realize she had made a promise. Based on her conversation with her husband, she set out to figure out how she could take 53 kids from the South Side of Chicago to show them Sweden.

Ingrid was a well-built blond with blue eyes that in addition to being charming refused to take no for an answer. I think her first step was to contact Expressen, a local newspaper in Stockholm, to solicit their help. The goal was to get them to run stories about the poor kids from the South Side of Chicago to build interest and get families to volunteer to open their homes for us to stay in. This was pretty risky because at the time she convinced them to run the story; she had not resolved how she was going to get us from the U.S. to Sweden. Her next step was to try to get a commitment from one of the Chicago based airlines with routes to Sweden, to provide a plane free of charge. After considerable wrangling and nail biting, Ingrid convinced the President of Pan-Am Airlines to donate the plane. Once this happened, the family that owned Carson Pirie Scott one of Chicago's larger department store chains volunteered to provide free clothing and things began to snowball. The last hurdle was to get the Chicago Board of Education to agree to allow us to be off from school for two weeks, which like everything else Ingrid handled.

While this was taking place the *Expressen* Newspaper in Stockholm was running stories daily and getting more families to volunteer. In addition to securing families they were working on a schedule of activities for our stay in Sweden. Unbeknownst to any of us, one of the activities they were working on (which had not been confirmed) was for us to meet the King of Sweden Gustav Adolf VI. In Chicago all the local newspapers, including the Sun Times, Chicago Tribune and the Chicago Defender, as well as *Jet* Magazine were running stories on our upcoming trip to Sweden. Even Mayor Richard J. Daley got involved and issued a proclamation appointing us as "Chicago's 53 Little Ambassadors" from the South Side of Chicago.

There was just as much, if not more excitement at home and in school about our going to Sweden. During December 1965, the month before we were scheduled to leave that was all anybody was talking about. I can safely say that this would be the first plane ride for 99 percent of the students. Our school, Forrestville High School, was especially proud because 24 of the 53 kids were from our school. The kids from our school included me, Derrick Agins, Helen Berry, Ivory Blisset, Mary Bordelon, Catherine Christian, Kevin Dixon, Howard Fitch, Lesly Flanagan, Helen Gallagher, Melvin Gatherwright, Robert Hayes, Carolyn Haynes, Sandra Hopkins, Hilda Keese, Milton Kennard, Bonnie McFarland, Dewitt Minyard, Francine Parret, Wanda Shade, Glendora Tatum, Jacqueline Watson, Cathy Williams and Valoris Woods.

The day we left, January 9, 1966, was one of the most exciting days of my life. I was so excited that I could barely contain myself and yet extremely apprehensive about the long flight. The funny thing about being excited for an extended period of time is it tends to exhaust you. By the time I got on the plane, and it took off, I was wiped out and fell asleep immediately. When we arrived in Stockholm, I had no idea what to expect. On the plane, each one of us was given a tag with our name and a number on it that would be used to identify us to our Swedish family waiting for us on the other side of customs. Ironically I was number 53. The morning we arrived it was bitter cold, unlike the kind of cold we were accustomed to; it was a wet penetrating type of cold. When we cleared customs it was a madhouse filled with news reporters, photographers flashing away and families desperately looking for the newest addition to their family from the South Side of Chicago.

My family was the Bergstroms who lived in a small suburban community south of Stockholm called Saltsjodaden. My parents were psychologists Agneta and Lennart Bergstrom. I had one sister, Gidrun, and three brothers, Leif, Lohern and Ludwig. Everyone was older than me except for Ludwig, who was around six or seven. They lived near a beautiful lake in a home that was everything Ingrid described as a typical home in Sweden. It was warm, nicely furnished, and most of all it was so clean you could eat off the floor. I later discovered that several of the other kids were living with famous families. One in particular, was Helen Berry,

82

who was living with Alice Babs, a famous Swedish singer. Alice Babs was like a Swedish version of Dinah Shore who had worked with a lot of the greats, including Duke Ellington.

Every morning I would get up and have breakfast with my family and then walk to the train station to catch the train into Stockholm to meet up with the rest of the group. Initially, one of my Swedish brothers or Gidrun would ride with me until I became comfortable taking the train on my own. Keep in mind they were still in school. We would meet at the *Expressen* Newspaper and leave from there going to whatever activity they had planned for us that day. Each day we did something different. One day we visited an area called "Old Town," which had narrow wavy cobblestone streets with plenty of small quaint and interesting shops along the way. It was one of Stockholm's biggest tourist attractions. You could find a lot of Swedish crystal and delicacies in many of the shops. Another well known attraction in Stockholm, we visited was the Wasa Museum. It housed the Wasa Vessel that sank in 1628 during its maiden voyage that was brought to the surface in 1961. We got to tour the vessel and learn all the details surrounding the sinking and retrieval of the vessel.

We also did a lot of sightseeing around Stockholm and had plenty of time to shop including at NK (Nordiska Kompaniet), one of Stockholm's largest and oldest department stores. It had a four-story center atrium much like the one in Macy's (formerly known as Marshall Fields) in downtown Chicago today. During our visit, we had several ski trips to the mountains where most of us attempted to learn to ski for the first time. In the evening, we would return home to have dinner with our host family if nothing was planned. On a number of occasions, when we went skiing and on the weekends, the activities would include them.

The biggest event of the trip was of course visiting Drottningholm Palace and meeting the King of Sweden, King Gustav Adolf VI. It was a fairy tale-like experience from beginning to end. Everyone was well groomed, impeccably dressed and on their best behavior. We had practiced for hours before we left the U.S. how to bow and curtsy properly. We were ready. After touring the palace we were assembled in one of the great halls to meet the King. The girls were lined up on one side and the boys on the other side. The King who arrived escorted by his staff was surprisingly tall, 6'2" or 6'3." He was first introduced to Dr. Kostrubala and his wife Ingrid by his staff. After curtsying, Ingrid spoke to the king in Swedish. He then turned to us, welcomed us to the palace and said he hoped we were enjoying our stay in his country and would always have fond memories. Dr. K. and Ingrid then introduced him to each one of us individually and we each bowed or curtsied at the appropriate time. The entire experience was remarkable and unforgettable.

Needless to say every one of us felt great and proud of having this opportunity. The trip from our perspective was a complete success, and we were living up to being "The 53 Little Ambassadors" from the South Side of Chicago. The press coverage in Sweden and throughout Europe was extremely positive as well as the coverage from the U.S. publications traveling with us with one exception. The photographer from *Look* Magazine repeatedly positioned several of the young men in suggestive poses with females from our host families. During a snow sledding event that included all the host families, the photographer talked Robert Hayes into getting into one of the sleds with a tall buxom blue-eyed blond Swedish young lady. I saw him trying to pose them in suggestive ways and immediately went to Charles Saunders and expressed my concerns. Charles Saunders was the Paris Editor for Johnson Publishing Company, publisher of *Ebony* and *Jet* Magazine. He was a large teddy bearlike guy who was always looking out for us. He immediately went with me to confront the photographer. He instructed Bob and the young lady to sit up in the sled and then told the photographer he knew what he was attempting to do. He threatened to expose what he was up to if he caught him doing it again. It never happened again and the photographer moved on.

The positive press we were receiving throughout Europe caused several other countries to invite us to visit them. The problem was it would require missing more school, and we needed to get back. However, it was decided that we could go to Copenhagen, Denmark for a brief stay before returning to the U.S. All I can remember about this portion of the trip was that I stayed with an American family instead of a Danish family. The husband was an expat that worked for General Motors. Like my Swedish family, they were great people. Unfortunately, I did not have as much time to get to know them. When we finally returned home, we were welcomed back like returning war heroes. We received commendations from local politicians and various organizations. We were invited by several different groups to come and share the experience with them. For the first 60 days back we were busy telling everybody about our trip.

Later in the school year after the excitement of the trip had begun to die down, Dr. Thompson made us aware of another opportunity. There was a new program called Upward Bound being launched at several universities around the country, including at Loyola University in Chicago. Dr. Thompson had been approached about a teaching position in the program. The purpose of the program was to provide students with college potential from disadvantaged backgrounds the preparation and support needed to insure their success in college. Students selected for the program would get to spend six weeks during the summer living on campus undergoing intense college prep. Deciding to participate in the program was a no-brainer, especially after being told it would help increase the chances of getting accepted into college. My mother was thrilled about the prospect of it helping me get in college and relieved that I would be spending the summer on campus instead of at home. At the end of my sophomore school year, I packed up my things and headed off to Loyola's North Shore campus. In addition to me: Dewitt Minyard, Derrick Agins, Lesly Flanagan, Bob Hayes, Leroy Ousley and John Douglas were also accepted in the program.

The first day was chaotic as we were introduced to the staff and the other students in the program. There were a lot of students (at least 100) in the program from high schools all over Chicago, including several Catholic schools. The boys definitely outnumbered the girls. It was like the United Nations with students from every ethnicity: White, Puerto Rican, Cuban, Mexican, African-American, Irish-American, Polish-American and Italian-American. Besides Dr. Thompson, we met several of the other instructors such as Alvin Lubov, Richard Nugent and Harold Pace as well as the director of the program, Dr. Barney Berlin and the assistant director, Bill Finch. They were all very dynamic and engaging like Anderson Thompson. We also met some of the counselors/chaperones that would be staying with us in the fraternity/sorority houses we used as dormitories, Bill Ware, Bob Corbin and Jeannie.

I was assigned to the TKE House, which was the Tau Kappa Epsilon's fraternity house, one of the world's largest college social fraternities in terms of the number of active groups. This was my first experience living away from home being with non-family members. One of my roommates who ultimately became a friend was a guy named Cornell Michael Preshon from Holy Name Cathedral High School. Initially, I was confused about his ethnicity because he looked slightly Hispanic. He was light-skinned with quasi curly hair. After he opened his mouth, I knew he was African-American. The guys who knew him from school called him "Posh." We called him Michael or by his last name. He was medium height with a stocky build and had a bad case of acne. He fancied himself a basketball player. Unfortunately, he had more heart than skill; this of course is coming from someone completely void of both. He was from the West Side of Chicago and lived with his Aunt Freda and his five younger siblings; Bernard, Cleveland, Lucille, Keith and Gregory.

In addition to Michael Preshon, we met and made friends with a lot of other kids. The most notable was Larry Waddell from Hales Franciscan High School. He hung out with a guy who attended school with him whose legal name was Hasan Ali that went by the name of Sam Ali. I think Sam was Iranian, but he behaved and spoke like he was African-American. He lived in the same neighborhood on 26th and Calumet with Larry, who we called Capon. Larry was very dark and tall, he stood about 6'3" or 6'4." He and Sam played basketball for Hales, which automatically made him friends with John Douglas. We got to know and hang out with Larry and Sam through John.

The most outrageous person we met at Upward Bound was Ransom "Cecil" Boykins. Cecil was from Wendell Phillips High School and as gay as you can be. He was completely out of the closet long before it was acceptable to be out. He was about Larry's height and weighed well over 300 pounds. He was light complexioned with flaming red hair and freckles. He was bright with great potential like everyone else. The only problem was that he was completely self-absorbed with being gay. On the weekends, he dressed in drag and performed on stage as a female impersonator. He wasn't a bad person once you got to know him but the problem was most people were too afraid of him to take the time.

In class, we dealt with issues the teachers thought might be problem areas that could potentially stand in our way of being successful in college. We spent time on the use of proper English; essay writing; techniques for increasing reading comprehension; skills for improving your performance on tests; adjusting to college life and picking college classes. We also spent time in class with Alvin Lubov delving into personal issues each one of us was faced with that could cause us to fail. He had a special ability to identify and draw out your weaknesses, forcing you to deal with them with his help of course. Classroom sessions with him were always intense but in the end very beneficial. We also went on a lot of trips to tour various college campuses, attended plays in the park and put on a play by Thornton Wilder called "The Skin of Our Teeth."

Mr. Bogan decided to top off the end of the semester by having the NYC throw a Christmas Dance. His idea was not to have one of our typical sweaty dances or sock hops in the gym. He wanted this to be a new experience for us, so he rented one of the smaller ballrooms at the Essex House hotel located in downtown Chicago for the dance, and everyone had to come dressed in after-five attire. As direct employees of the NYC we were all expected to attend. The problem for me was who I was going to take. Over the summer, I had just met a girl who was a friend of Derrick's younger sister Cynthia Agins. We hung out a lot at Derrick's house during the summer. Cynthia had mentioned to me once before that she had a girlfriend who didn't go to school with us that I might like. Her girlfriend's name was Bunny, and she lived in Stateway Gardens. The fact that she lived in Stateway Gardens was an immediate turn-off. Stateway had a reputation for being dangerous for outsiders and especially for guys trying to date their girls. The day I met Bunny whose real name was Rita Sutton, I realized I had seen her before. I saw her a couple of times when I went to collect for the newspaper from her grandfather, Mr. Clarence Sutton, who lived two doors down from the Agins family. She was light-skinned with long jet-black hair and big legs. She looked as if she were Hispanic but in talking to her, you quickly realized that was not the case. She spoke in a slight down-home manner, as if she was from the South, which was not the case. The other thing that was striking about her was her nurturing spirit. At the time I had no idea what a nurturing spirit was; all I knew was that there was something different about her. I asked her to go to the NYC Christmas Dance with me, and she said yes provided her parents agreed. I went to meet her parents and ended up having to ask her mother if she could attend the dance with me. She said yes after giving me the third degree and letting me know that I needed to treat her daughter like a lady at all times. In the end, I was more frightened asking her mother for permission than asking her daughter.

The rest of my junior year and senior year were relatively uneventful compared to the events of 1966. The Magnificent 7 was still active, traveling and performing at different schools and events. I continued to do well in school and was on track for becoming a solid B student. In fact, I was elected senior class president. I attribute a lot of this to the positive impact the Upward Bound program was having on me. During the school year, we attended classes on Saturday at Lewis Towers, Loyola's downtown campus. In the summer, we went back to live in the dorms on the north shore campus. From the experience with Upward Bound, I decided I wanted to apply to Loyola for college and was accepted. It is safe to say that not only did my grades improve during this time but so did my popularity and dating. Even though I had several options, I decided to take Bunny (Rita) to my Senior Prom. There was something special about her. As we were finalizing plans for the prom, I asked her what color dress was she wearing to determine what color tuxedo jacket to rent and corsage to purchase. She went on to tell me that it was a peach, cream and green plaid satin dress. When she described the dress, I became alarmed because it did not sound anything like the pastel colored chiffon dresses that I knew all the other girls would be wearing. For a brief moment, I was almost tempted to come up with an excuse for backing out of taking her to my prom. I am glad I didn't because the dress was absolutely stunning, and she looked gorgeous. She was truly the bell of the ball, and I received tons of compliments on how beautiful she looked.

#

When I look back on this time in my life the best way to describe it is a period of enrichment and blessings for the foundation of many things to come in my life was being laid.

Psalm 128: 1-3 reminds us: "Blessed are all who fear the LORD, who walk in His ways. You will eat the fruit of your labor; blessings and prosperity will be yours. Your wife will be like a fruitful vine within your house; your sons will be like olive shoots around your table."

Psalm 84:11-12 says: "For the LORD God is a sun and shield; the LORD bestows favor and honor; no good thing does He withhold from those whose walk is blameless. LORD Almighty, blessed is the man who trusts in You."

Trip to Sweden

King Gustav Adolf VI

Ingrid and Dr. Kostrubala chatting with the king

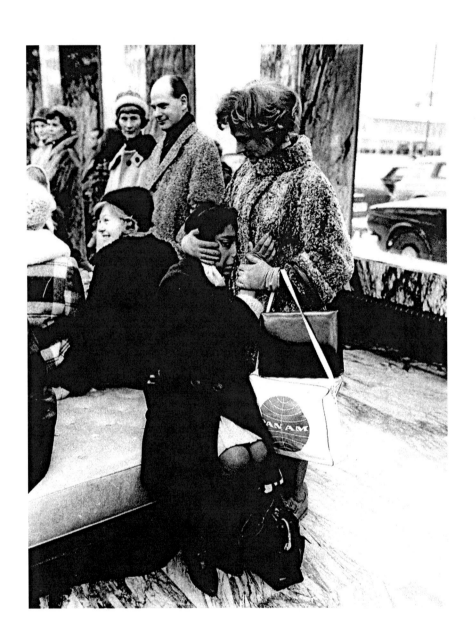

Forrestville High School

Eugene Bogan

Senior Class Officers

97

The Prom

Rita Frances Sutton

Some
Enchanted
Evening

SENIOR CLASS OFFICERS

President .... Alvin Jackson
Vice-President .... Carolyn Haynes
Secretary .... Antoinette Woods
Treasurer .... Earlene Roberts
Business Manager ...... Lesley Flanagan

SENIOR SPONSORS

Mrs. Shirley Andrews
Mr. William Hunter

CLASS COLORS
Black and Gold

PROM COMMITTEE

Barbara Bohanon
Lesley Flanagan
Helen Gallagher
Lucy Hammond
Shirley Hines
Evelyn McCane
Aldine Parker
Glendora Tatum
Sandra Thomas

S is for the Stars, like brilliant
   sparkling rock

E is for my Escort *Alvin*
   who came at *8.00* o'clock.

N is for the Night and the air, so
   fresh and sweet

I is for Ideal, a night that can't be
   beat

O is for the Orchestra that played
   throughout the night

R is for our Rapture, as to *Pick Congress* our path led

P is for Pretty my *Pink + orch:*
   corsage, lovely and just right

R is for Remembering the *Good*
   fun time I had that night

O is for *5.00 A.M.* O'clock
   the time we got back home

M is for the Memories inscribed
   within this poem.

Going to College – the Wake-up Call that Caught Me Off Guard

Being accepted to attend Loyola University of Chicago was good, but I really wanted to go to Fisk University in Nashville, Tennessee or one of the other historically Black colleges (HBCs). I was offered a partial scholarship to Fisk, which would have required considerable loans to cover the difference. My mother was adamant that I should attend Loyola; her position was that if it was good enough for Mayor Daley's son it was good enough for me. In the end, I acquiesced because it was a good school; the scholarships I was offered to Loyola made it affordable and Fisk was just too costly and far away. Several of my friends from Forrestville High School were also accepted at Loyola such as Dewitt Minyard, John Douglas and Lesly Flanagan as well as a couple from Upward Bound like Mike Preshon and Larry Waddell. Many of the others, including Derrick Agins, Bob Hayes and Leroy Ousley went to a junior college in Evanston, Illinois called Kendall College. Kendall was a 20-minute ride by car from Loyola.

When I arrived at Loyola, I thought I was prepared for college life. Unlike most of the other freshmen, I had spent the past three summers on the campus and knew my way around. Besides, Upward Bound had taught me what to expect and how to deal with it. This could not be farther from the truth. I soon discovered that my experience with Upward Bound was tantamount to riding a bike with training wheels. I now found myself on a 10-speed racer up against some of the best speed racers in the city. The other problem I faced was I had not learned how to balance my time between studying and socializing.

As a freshman I was required to stay in one of the freshmen dorms. I ended up in Campion Hall with Mike Preshon from Upward Bound as my roommate. Through the time spent at Upward Bound, Mike and I had become friends. Campion Hall was a three-story building located on Sheridan Road. Mike and I were in room 242. In many ways Mike and I were complete opposites. I was neat and organized, and he was junky and not very focused. We fought constantly about him leaving his things all over the room, especially his funky gym shoes on the window ledge to air out, which, by the way, was on my side of the room. One of the things that we did share in common was the importance of finishing college. We would be the first in our families to go to college and receive a college degree. We both wanted to major in psychology so that we could help others. I am sure this had a lot to do with the dysfunctional nature of our family experiences. Mike lived with his Aunt Freda and his younger siblings instead of with his mom. His mom was known for drinking and running off behind some man and leaving the kids, which is why his aunt had custody.

Even though Loyola was predominantly a White school the doctrine of separate but equal was in full play. For the most part, the White kids hung out with each other, and the Black kids hung out with other Black kids. The extent of our interacting was in the classrooms and at sports activities. The other Black kids at Loyola were from all over. A lot were from Chicago and the neighboring cities and states. Since Loyola was a Jesuit College a lot of them came from Catholic schools. However, I was surprised at the number of students from New York many of which were athletes. What I did not realize at the time was that the Athletic Department did a lot of recruiting in New York for basketball and track. Loyola did not have a football team. I was told that there was an accident and a student was severely injured and the school discontinued the football program. As for basketball and track Loyola had a history of doing well. Loyola's basketball team was the 1963 NCAA Champs under Coach George Ireland.

Some of the guys from New York who played basketball were Sol McMillian, Frank Peyton and Walt Robinson. The two guys from New York on the track team were Sid Mordant and Kenny Austin. Sol and Frank were power forwards on the basketball team and Walt Robinson was the team's star guard and highest scorer. Sol had drug connections and Frank was a gambler. Walt was strictly into playing ball other than a little recreational indulgence. The three were typical New Yorkers. Sid and Kenny were from Jamaica, New York and more down to earth. Sid was thin and about my height with a huge infectious smile and engaging personality. He was funny and likeable. Kenny did not look like a track star; he was more muscular and looked as if he could have been a wrestler. He was cool and easy going.

My first year of school was spent trying to keep up in class after I discovered that I could not B.S. my way through and trying to keep up socially. As hard as I tried, I always felt that I was failing at both. Academically I was falling behind because I didn't realize that you needed to devote twice or three times as much time studying and preparing for class to stand a chance of keeping up in class. Somehow I was under the grand illusion that all I had to do was show up and participate in class. It helped but it was far from being enough to be anything more than a D or C student. Socially, I didn't know whether I wanted to be cool and hang out with the fellas who were considered cool or be a nerd. Most of my friends from Forrestville and the guys from New York fell in the category of being cool. They hung out a lot at the pool room across from the dorm or in the basement watching TV when they were not getting high or playing basketball. The one thing they did not seem to do at all was study. Having Mike Preshon as my roommate helped a little. Unlike everyone else, he did not drink, smoke cigarettes or get high. He played a little basketball, which helped prevent him from being labeled a nerd. I split my time between hanging out with the fellas and doing things with Mike.

When I was hanging out with the fellas much of that time was with Sid. Beneath the New York exterior Sid was really a nice guy. One time we were talking about the difference between Chicagoans and New Yorkers. Sid liked folks from Chicago because he said they were a lot friendlier than New Yorkers. I had never been to New York but disagreed because I knew Chicagoans could be distant and stand-offish. He came up with a contest and he and I went to the corner of State Street and Madison, the heart of downtown Chicago. Sid, who was wearing a hat, would tip his hat and say hello, and it was my job to count the number of people who responded to him. Later in the year during school break he invited me to go home with him to New York. We went into Manhattan, stood directly in front of Bloomingdale's and did the same thing. Instead of responding back most people just ignored us. He won the bet.

The other diversion was chasing the ladies. I was chasing a young lady name Dorothy Quarles, who attended Kendall College. Dorothy and I met and started dating at Upward Bound. She was from the Wentworth Garden projects and attended Wendell Phillips High School. We had what I called a summer relationship meaning we dated only during the summer when we were at Upward Bound. We started dating casually at the end of the first summer of the program. We did not see each other much during the regular school year, except on Saturday when we attended Upward Bound classes at Lewis Tower. Dorothy was tan complexioned and medium height for a girl, with short hair and a bit on the chubby side, but she was a great dancer, and I loved to dance. Our relationship became closer during my senior year when she lost her mother and had to move in with her older sister who lived in Hyde Park. Her sister was gay and lived with her domestic partner, which was a whole new experience for me. In any case, I spent a lot of time on the weekend traveling back and forward to Kendall to see Dorothy instead of studying.

Back on campus when I hung out with Mike a lot of our time together involved me trying to help him pursue Jacqueline Watson. I knew Jackie from Forrestville High School. She was in many of my classes and friends with the other "smart girls" in school that we were often paired with. Jackie was very attractive. She was a brown-skinned, petite yet very shapely girl with pretty hair and a great smile. In high school several of my friends (Leroy and Lesly) and even I wanted to date her. None of us did because she came from a very religious and strict family with a mother who kept a very tight rein on her and her sisters. To be honest about it, I did not think that Mike had a snowball's chance in hell to date Jackie. Nevertheless, he was my friend and roommate, so I had no choice but to help him. Jackie lived at the Edgewater Beach Hotel, which had been converted into a temporary dorm while they were waiting to complete construction of Mertz Hall.

There were several other Black girls living at Edgewater Beach that Jackie had become friends with including Shirley Bennett, Delores Lattimore, Gloria Jenkins, Karen Brown, Midge Sinclair, Deborah Ward, Peggy Edison, Norvella Reed and Cecilia Jackson. After numerous visits to Edgewater, a little help from me sprucing up his game and his unwillingness to accept no for an answer, his relentless pursuit paid off, and Jackie started dating Michael. It was a surprise to everyone (especially the guys from Forrestville) and no one predicted it would last long. I am proud to say they got married in 1970 and are still married today. During the process of helping Mike, I got to know most of the girls and started dating one of them named Shirley Bennett. Shirley also attended Forrestville High School but was dating a guy named Orval O'Neal. They broke up after high school. She was brown-skinned like Jackie with a killer smile and nice shape. The problem with Shirley was that she was confused. She liked all the attention I was showering on her, but unbeknownst to me, secretly had a crush on Larry Waddell (Capon) and didn't know what to do about it. She eventually broke things off with me when she thought she had a chance at dating Larry, which unfortunately for her never happened.

Shortly after dating Shirley, I started talking with one of the other girls from Edgewater Beach. In the beginning it was, as if she was trying to console me after the breakup with Shirley. Her name was Karen Brown. She grew up on 95th and Champlain and attended Harlan High School. She was medium complexion, buxom and about my height. She was in a couple of my classes and seemed to be somewhat shy and stuttered a little. I soon discovered this was definitely not the case. She was only shy speaking in public. One-on-one or in more comfortable settings she had something to say about most things. In many was we were very different. I was popular and outgoing, whereas she was quiet and somewhat withdrawn. I was attracted to the limelight, and she shied away from it.

At the end of my freshmen year I was carrying a GPA of less than 2.0 and placed on academic probation. I rationalized to myself that it was just the challenge of getting acclimated to the academic rigor of college course work, and that I would do better next year. I also forgot to mention that during my freshmen year, the fall of 1968, my son Richard was born. I entered my second year of college committed to improving my grades and now that I had a son I definitely needed to do better. In spite of my renewed commitment, I continued to struggle. The course work was getting progressively harder and the things I did not learn in my freshmen year were coming back to haunt me. Many of the classes I was taking were a continuation of the introductory classes and built on what I should have learned in my freshmen year. I was drowning from the cumulative effect of what I did not retain as a freshman. The weight of it all came crashing in on me at the end of my sophomore year. I received a letter indicating I could not return to school in the fall because I had failed to meet academic standards by maintaining a minimum GPA of 2.0. I was devastated and did not know what to do.

I went to see Dr. Barney Berlin, the head of the Loyola Upward Bound Program who was on staff at Loyola. He was the Department Head of the School of Education. We talked for a long time as I tried to explain to him why I was failing. I was very candid with him about all the partying and failing to study. I told him that I had just become a father. I also told him that I did not think psychology was for me, and that I wanted to switch to business. He was equally disappointed in me and agreed to help me, if I gave him my word that I was going to change and knuckle down and become the serious student he knew I could be. I gave him my word, and he went to the Dean of Admissions. He got him to agree to let me return in the fall as a night student, enrolled in the School of Continuing Education, provided, I made up two of the courses I failed with no less than a B in each class. If I managed to do that he would approve me taking up to six credit hours during the day through the School of Education and six credit hours in the evening as a continuing education student.

That summer I went home and told my mother what happened. She didn't have to say a word because I could see her disappointment written all across her face. For the next couple of days, she did not say a word. Finally, she said to me that I had one chance to get myself back on track, and if I didn't I was going to have to find someplace else to stay. She went on to say that in addition to the requirements the school had placed on me that I needed to find a job during the summer to support myself. On top of having to pass the two classes with no less than a B, I was also going to have to find a job. I felt like things could not get any worse. After signing up to take the two classes and completely re-doing my room at home, so that it would be more conducive to studying, I went looking for a job. I started by doing all the usual things like checking the want ads and going to the Urban League. I was not having much luck and got the bright idea that maybe I should try to find a job at a company like Johnson Publishing Company. I was reading the *Jet* Magazine and saw a picture of Charles Saunders, who I met on the trip to Sweden. From the article and photo, I could tell he was back in the U.S.

The next day I got dressed and took the bus down to Johnson Publishing Company, located at 1820 South Michigan. Johnson Publishing Company was located in what had previously been a large mortuary. They had completely remodeled the building and turned it into a very nice office space. Ruth Wagner was at the reception desk and asked how she could help me. I told her I was here to see Mr. Charles Saunders. She asked if I had an appointment, and I said no. Then she asked my name and proceeded to call Mr. Saunders. When she gave him my name, at first he did not recognize it and asked what this was all about. I proceeded to tell her that I had met him in Sweden, and that I was one of the 53 students who took the trip to Sweden and met the King. She conveyed this back to Charles, and he told her to have me wait. About two minutes later he walked toward me in the reception area, shook my hand and gave me a big hug. We chatted for a little while before I indicated to him that I needed a job and reminded him that he told me in Sweden if I ever needed his help to just let him know. He asked how school was, and I told him what was going on. He appreciated my being honest. He said, "Let me see what I can do. I will talk with the head of personnel, LaDoris Foster, to see if there is anything available." A week later I got a call from Miss. Foster asking me to come in to meet with Mrs. Lavada McGhee about a position in their shipping department. I got the job.

The summer of 1970 was truly a new beginning for me; it marked the beginning of me getting my life back on track. I did well with the two courses I took and ended up with a B+ in one and an A in the other one. Working for Johnson Publishing Company was great. I worked in the shipping department in the area responsible for shipping out wigs. I did not realize that in addition to publishing *Ebony, Jet* and *Negro Digest* that the company sold a lot of other products, one of which was wigs. The product was called Star Glow Wigs, which came in an assortment of styles and colors. It was my job to process the orders, most of which were for a single wig. The wigs were stored upstairs on the second floor in a wide-open space in the back of the building. The area was in complete disarray. I am assuming when the wigs came in the drivers would just dump them upstairs. Every time I would go upstairs to get the wigs needed to fill orders it would take forever to find the right wigs in terms of style and color. I decided that I needed to organize the area, which was the size of a high school gymnasium. I didn't tell Mrs. McGhee or the lady I worked with, Shirley, what I wanted to do. Instead I told the guard that I needed to come in on the weekend to organize the inventory upstairs. He said fine and that he would let the weekend security person know that I was coming in. I completely reorganized the area putting the wigs of like style and color in the same area. I used masking tape to mark off the floor. I also wrote on the masking tape the name of each wig along with the style and color that was stored in that section.

The following week and subsequent weeks filling orders was easy, and it took a lot less time. Mrs. McGhee and Shirley noticed that it was taking me a lot less time to process orders. When they asked why, I just said I had a new system and let it go. At the end of summer, on my last day, Mrs. McGhee came over to thank me for doing a great job and wish me well. She gave me my last pay check and told me that Mr. Johnson wanted to see me. Throughout the entire summer working for the company, I had never met Mr. Johnson. I would see him around the building occasionally and most of the time I would see him coming and going in his black chauffeur driven Cadillac limousine. I went to see Mr. Johnson, who had this huge office at the front of the building on the second floor. He asked me how I enjoyed working for the company, and I said I enjoyed it a lot. He went on to proceed to tell me that everyone around the building thought I was a nice young man and that Mrs. McGhee especially appreciated my hard work and dedication. They were both aware that I came in on a Saturday and spent the entire day rearranging the wigs and never once asked to be paid for the time I spent doing it. He then handed me an envelope and told me to come back next summer, and that he would find me something else to do. I left the building right after meeting him and did not open the envelope until I was on the bus and was pleasantly surprised to see it was a check for $500.00.

In the fall, I returned to school enrolled in two classes in the School of Education and two classes in the evening through the School of Continuing Education. Instead of living in a dorm, I was back at home in a room half the size of my old dorm room. It did not matter to me because all I was planning on doing was sleeping and studying in the room. When I needed more space, I would study at the school library. I finished the first semester with three A's and one B. I went back to Dr. Barney Berlin with my grades, and he said, "Now that you have proven you are serious let's see what we can do to get you back in school as a full time student," which he was able to do. The next semester, I registered as a full time student in the School of Business. I took six courses for a total of 18 credit hours and finished the semester with a 3.5 GPA for the semester.

The following summer I went to summer school again and took two classes as well as returned to work for Johnson Publishing Company. This time instead of working in the shipping department, I went to work for Supreme Beauty Products (another company, he owned) that sold hair care products to beauticians, barbers and retailers. Supreme was located at 645 North Michigan not far from Lewis Tower, the downtown campus of Loyola, where I attended classes at the School of Business. Supreme Beauty Products was run by Shirley Calloway, who was White. The rest of the management team was Black and consisted of Pat Johnson, the

General sales manager and Lance Clarke, who was the manager of retail sales. The sales staff consisted of Mr. Dumas, Sonja Lavender, Sandra Luster and Tina Lewis. I was assigned to calling on the professional trades, barbers and beauticians to sell them Duke and Raveen Hair Care products.

When I returned to school in the fall of 1971, I aggressively continued trying to get back on track in hopes of graduating with the class I came in with. The next two semesters I took classes totaling 21 credit hours each semester even though I was beginning to feel a little burnt out. By now I was hanging out with Al Lawrence, who, like me, was a business student majoring in accounting, while I was working on a dual major in marketing and HR. We had several classes together and often studied together. I did not make my goal of getting all of my course work completed so that I could finish with my incoming class. I was nine credit hours short of the requirement to graduate. I later completed the requirements and did receive my degree from Loyola in business administration.

#

I entered college with great hope and promise, and somehow I got lost in self-indulgence. I allowed my transgressions and desire to overshadow my purpose and goals.

Ephesians 2: 1-10 says: "As for you, you were dead in your transgressions and sins, in which you used to live when you followed the ways of this world and of the ruler of the kingdom of the air, the spirit who is now at work in those who are disobedient. All of us also lived among them at one time, gratifying the cravings of our sinful nature and following its desires and thoughts. Like the rest, we were by nature objects of wrath. But because of his great love for us, God, who is rich in mercy, made us alive with Christ even when we were dead in transgressions — it is by grace you have been saved. And God raised us up with Christ and seated us with him in the heavenly realms in Christ Jesus, in order that in the coming ages he might show the incomparable riches of his grace, expressed in his kindness to us in Christ Jesus. For it is by grace you have been saved, through faith—and this not from yourselves, it is the gift of God — not by works, so that no one can boast. For we are God's workmanship, created in Christ Jesus to do good works, which God prepared in advance for us to do."

Loyola University of Chicago
Dumbach and Cudahy Hall

CHAPTER 3

READY!.....SET!.....GO!

Marriage, the Roller Coaster Ride that Left Me Crying Instead of Laughing

My relationship with Karen Brown started off rocky. We were in an English literature class together and each student was required to stand up and provide comments. Karen was extremely nervous when it came time for her to speak, and she stuttered when she spoke. She caught Mike Preshon and I laughing and sneered at us. For a long time, she would not speak to either of us when she saw us. She would just give us the look that said she thought we were disgusting. It wasn't until Michael starting dating Jackie and Shirley broke it off with me that she began having anything to do with us. That's why I was surprised when she attempted to console me after the breakup with Shirley. Initially, I thought she was doing it as a prank, or it was her way of getting back for laughing at her. It turns out; she was being sincere and was just trying to break out of her shell.

By now the girls from Edgewater Beach had moved on campus, directly across from Campion Hall into the new dorm Mertz Hall in suite 13B. During my last semester at school on campus this made it easy for us to see each other on a regular basis, which we did. In fact, when I got the news that I was not going to be able to return to school in the fall because of my grades, she was the first person I talked with to help figure out what I needed to do. I think we started dating because most of the other Black girls who lived in the suite with her (the same ones from Edgewater Beach) had begun dating my friends. Jackie Watson was dating Michael Preshon; Delores Lattimore was dating Dewitt Minyard; Gloria Jenkins was semi-dating John Douglas and Shirley Bennett was trying to date Capon. Karen and I were the only two not dating someone from each other's respective group of friends. It stood to reason that we should start dating. Everybody else on campus would make jokes about the brothers from Campion Hall dating the girls from "Suite 13B."

111

Karen was an education major and was very studious. She took studying and going to class very seriously. She did not party and was not into drinking or drugs. For me that was part of what attracted me to her. I realized even before getting the letter that I needed to buckle down and get serious about school. I could feel the opportunity slipping away from me. Dating Karen gave me an excuse for not hanging out with the fellas, and, I was hoping, an opportunity to spend more time studying. We would go to the library together but unfortunately for me, it was too late to reverse things.

It wasn't long after I started dating Karen that I realized she was very jealous, and not just of other girls, but of anyone I spent time with other than her. There were also signs that she was not very good at managing her anger. She would easily get upset and fly into a rage about things that I considered small. The other thing that I didn't see as a problem was her attachment to her family. It later proved to be a big one. She had three older sisters, Janice McKenzie, Yvonne Thompson and Cynthia Harris, and two younger siblings Steve and Pam. Her mother Norma Avery, two younger siblings and grandmother (everyone called her "Big Mama") lived in a two-family brick house that was owned by her grandmother on 95th and Champlain. Her mother and older sisters were all LPNs and worked at hospitals or as private duty nurses through a nursing registry. As a family they were tight-knit and could be very volatile at times. Janice was a bourgeoisie wannabe; Yvonne was easygoing and loveable; Cynthia was a firecracker with a short fuse and Steve and Pam were cute little kids. They were both light-skinned with a very nice grade of hair and looked very different from the rest of the family. They did not have the same father as Karen and her older sisters. Steve and Pam's father was Asian. Her mother, who I truly liked, was misunderstood and condemned for wanting to find love. Big Mama was a hell raiser plain and simple.

Janice was married to Calvin McKenzie, a tall and thin medium-complexioned brother from the South. Calvin was a good guy who was very handy and could pretty much fix or do anything he set his mind to doing. He taught science at Lindblom, a high school on the South Side of Chicago, and it seemed like he spent all of his time working on cars when he was not teaching. Janice, who was the same complexion as Calvin, was short and on the chubby side. Her favorite pastimes were shopping and telling everybody else what to do. Her claim to fame, according to her, was she dated Harold Ford, Sr., the former congressman from Tennessee and the father of former Congressman Harold Ford Jr. who succeeded him. She also knew and was friends with someone in Senator Edward Brooke's family.

Yvonne and Greg and their son Stephen lived across the street from Karen's family. Yvonne worked hard. She was gone most of the time and tended to keep to herself. She seemed to be closer to Big Mama than her mother. Her husband Greg enjoyed listening to his music and getting high. He wasn't big on socializing with the rest of the family and pretty much stayed to himself most of the time. Cynthia and Terry Harris were younger and had three kids (Brenda, Bernadette and Olushia). They loved partying and getting high. Cynthia was about 5'6" tall and Terry was 6'8." Terry played basketball in high school and college but was not good enough to be drafted into the pros. They lived in the South Shore area and drove a 1971 Buick Electra 225 convertible. Most of the time Terry was out of work and earned money hustling. His lack of a job made him one of Janice's least favored and was the source of many fights with his wife Cynthia. When they fought it was dangerous because even with the difference in size, Cynthia would go toe-to-toe with him. It would normally end with someone having to call the police to get her off of him.

Karen's mother was a shade lighter than her and had red hair. Most would describe her as an attractive, full-bosomed shapely woman.

When she wasn't working hard (which she did a lot), she was playing hard and enjoying herself. She enjoyed socializing with Seamen (her common-law husband) and their friends. They owned a powerboat and drove a 1972 Buick Electra 225 convertible. The house had a completely finished basement with a large well stocked bar. They entertained frequently and enjoyed living the good life, which they did most of the time, except when Seamen was suffering with gout.

Big Mama, who lived upstairs on the second floor, knew everybody in the neighborhood both young and old. When she and her husband bought the house, they were the first Black family to move into the neighborhood. She loved being in the middle of the action in the neighborhood and in the house. She would sit on the front porch drinking her Miller High Life beer, smoking Camel cigarettes and chatting with everybody that walked by. When she ran out of cigarettes or beer she was forever asking someone to go to the liquor store. During the holidays, she was known for starting to drink early and ending up drunk. When she got drunk you knew she was going to do something crazy. One time when this happened someone was mixing up their special barbecue sauce recipe in a big washtub. She got mad because no one was paying her any attention and took off her shoes and stepped into the barbecue sauce.

Now back to Karen and me. We continued to date after I left campus and in her senior year, she moved back home. As i was to be expected Karen graduated from Loyola slightly ahead of time with a degree in education. From the time, I left school until when I completed the requirements for my degree, she was instrumental in keeping me focused and for that I will always be eternally grateful. After Karen finished school and while I was in the process of finishing, we decided to get married. I bought a ring and we announced our engagement. We were in love and with school just about behind us; it seemed to be the logical thing to do. Besides several of our friends from school had already gotten married;

Michael married Jackie and Dewitt married Delores. The wedding was planned for November 25, 1972.

I had not given much thought to what I wanted in a wedding, so my expectations were fairly limited. Like most women Karen had been dreaming about her wedding for some time. It seemed that from the moment, we announced our plans to get married that her sister Janice went into overdrive. The first decision that had to be made was when and where. Karen and I had decided that it was going to be in the fall sometime in October or November. The exact date was going to depend of course on the availability of the facility. I don't recall how we ended up choosing the Beverly House, but we did. At the time I think it was one of the nicest facilities available on the South Side and the other option of going downtown was definitely too expensive. Since Karen and I were paying for the wedding money was an issue. Every other decision made regarding the wedding from this point on seemed to be influenced by Janice. I always had the feeling that she was working behind the scenes manipulating Karen into doing things her way and not just according to etiquette. She had assumed the role of the mother of the bride. When we got married, we had a huge wedding party consisting of thirteen bridesmaids and groomsmen. Except for my cousin Silvia, the bridesmaids included her sisters and most of the girls from suite 13B. The groomsmen were my friends from high school and college as well as my younger brother Tyrone and her brother Steve. The reception at the Beverly House was a sit-down dinner with an open bar. Everybody was invited including extended family; friends from the neighborhood where we grew up and tons of acquaintances from Loyola. It was quite the production.

Before we got married, we selected our apartment at 8916 South Justine, and I had already moved in. The one thing I made sure of was that it was not too close to her mother's house or where Janice lived. We lived on the southwest side of Chicago, and they lived southeast. From her

115

mother's house, it was a 15-20 minute drive and at least 35 minutes away from Janice. Our apartment was in a relatively new building in the neighborhood facing the commuter train tracks. Being near the tracks was not a problem because the front yard of the building, plus an empty lot and a small street separated us from the tracks. The building was a three story building with an English basement. We lived on the first floor in a two-bedroom apartment. Our living room had a large picture window, and the kitchen had modern appliances and an eat-in kitchen area. It was definitely a nice first apartment for a young couple. I was working downtown at Johnson Publishing Company selling advertising space in *Ebony* Magazine, and Karen was teaching at an all White school located northwest of where we lived, near Midway Airport.

The first year of the marriage had the typical ups and downs that are to be expected. We fought about the usual things, but we also seemed to fight a lot about doing things with anyone outside of her family and Michael and Jackie. She didn't seem to like or trust anyone else including my family and other friends. I was beginning to feel isolated. It was the source of a lot of our arguments, which were becoming more and more heated. When we argued she refused to back down or back away. When I would try to leave to get some air she would become even more aggressive.

After two years of marriage, we decided it was time to buy a house. We looked at different areas and decided we wanted to buy a home in the Beverly Hills area that was slightly southwest of where we lived. Beverly Hills to this day is an inter-racial community made up of approximately 60 percent White, 30 percent Black and 3 percent Hispanic. It is the third safest and wealthiest neighborhood in Chicago. It is known for its large homes, especially along Longwood Drive. It was home to notable Blacks such as Buddy Guy, Greg and Bryant Gumbel, Louis Farrakhan and Muhammad Ali's family. We bought a small (1,200 sq. foot) tri-level home

116

on 107th and Drew built in 1964. Most of the other homes on Drew were much older and larger. It was the perfect home for us; it was in a great neighborhood; on a large wooded lot and was a newer versus older home.

In spite of seemingly having it all, things seemed to be getting progressively worse. The arguments escalated to full-blown fights. The family involvement was reaching a level of being suffocating. Janice had a plan for everyone and was becoming increasingly more involved in everyone's life. She wanted her husband Calvin to leave teaching and become a doctor, which he did. He became a dentist. I was supposed to become a lawyer, which didn't happen because I had no interest. According to Janice, Yvonne needed to put her foot down with her husband Greg and give him an ultimatum to get a job or leave. He eventually left on his own. Cynthia and Terry (her husband) needed to grow up and become responsible parents and stop getting high. Unlike Karen, Cynthia didn't care what Janice thought or wanted. Her mother needed to stop feeling like she had to have a man. Big Mama needed to stop drinking Miller High Life beer and clowning. Steve and Pam were to finish high school and get into a good college and become professionals. She had a plan for everybody except for herself.

While all of this was going on, I was increasingly feeling the need for more change in my life. I had already left Johnson Publishing Company and was working for the 3M Company in the printing products' division. It wasn't long after I started working for 3M that I realized this was not a good fit, especially with everything else that was going on in my life. Karen had drifted farther away from me and more toward her family. She eventually hired an attorney and filed for divorce. I moved out of the house into the YMCA and started the process of seriously interviewing. I did it in the hope that I would find something that would give me the fresh start I felt I desperately needed.

117

#

As much as we want to believe that loving each other is the key to a successful marriage, it takes more. One of the most difficult aspects of marriage that most women struggle with is submitting to their husband and letting go of their families.

Ephesians 5: 21-33 tells us: "Submit to one another out of reverence for Christ. Wives, submit to your husbands as to the Lord. For the husband is the head of the wife as Christ is the head of the church, his body, of which he is the Savior. Now as the church submits to Christ, so also wives should submit to their husbands in everything.

"Husbands, love your wives, just as Christ loved the church and gave himself up for her to make her holy, cleansing her by the washing with water through the word, and to present her to himself as a radiant church, without stain or wrinkle or any other blemish, but holy and blameless. In this same way, husbands ought to love their wives as their own bodies. He who loves his wife loves himself. After all, no one ever hated his own body, but he feeds and cares for it, just as Christ does the church; for we are members of His body. For this reason, a man will leave his father and mother and be united to his wife, and the two will become one flesh."

This is a profound mystery—but I am talking about Christ and the church. However, each one of you also must love his wife as he loves himself, and the wife must respect her husband.

A Firsthand View of Greatness and Black Royalty

Prior to getting married with all but nine credit hours required to secure my degree, which I intended to pursue through the Continuing Education program, I decided it was time to find a job. In the spring of 1972, I began looking for full-time employment. I started attending the career fairs set up by the school with my buddy Al Lawrence, as well as sending out resumes. Most of the larger companies based in Chicago participated in Loyola's Career Fair, so it gave me an opportunity to meet with different companies. I quickly learned that the entry-level positions being offered to marketing or personnel majors were in sales or supervision. The only truly marketing related jobs were with the ad agencies, and you had to know someone to just get an interview. I wasn't having much luck even finding a sales position. The only real prospect I had was with Skil Corporation, a company that manufactured small professional hand tools. They were looking for someone to work in their Production Department supervising employees (primarily females) working on the assembly line.

One day I was attending a job fair put on by a company at the Conrad Hilton hotel located at 720 South Michigan Avenue. As I was walking in the lobby of the hotel about to leave, I saw Mr. Johnson walking in my direction. We spoke and he asked me how I was doing and what I was doing. I told him I was at a job fair. He replied "I thought you were going to come see me when you finished school." I responded that I had just started looking. He chuckled and said, "Keep looking and come see me before you accept an offer." I promised I would and left. I kept looking and the only offer I received was from Skil Corporation. I was not excited about the offer, because the last thing I wanted to do was be a Production Supervisor. Many of my friends from business school, including Al, had received offers. Al, who majored in accounting, got an offer from IBM. Dorothy Ragsdale, another friend of ours from business school received an offer from one of the steel companies. Disappointed with the offer from Skil, I called and set up an appointment to see Mr. Johnson.

Somehow in the midst of taking 21 credit hours each semester for the past two semesters, I did not realize that Johnson Publishing Company had moved into a brand new building. The new building was located at 820 South Michigan Avenue: next door to the Conrad Hilton hotel. The official grand opening of the building was May 16, 1972. When I arrived at the building in June, I was blown away by the exquisiteness of the 11-story building. The exterior of the building was made up of travertine marble and huge glass windows framed in a bronze material. The building was designed by a Black architect, John Moutoussamy. I went to Loyola with his son Claude and through him knew his daughter Jeannie, who later married Arthur Ashe. When I met with Mr. Johnson, he asked how the job-hunting was coming. I told him that I was nearing the end of it, and that I had received an offer from Skil Corporation. I gave him a copy of the offer letter that I received. He excused himself, came back with LaDoris Foster and said, "She will talk to you about a position with us." I left with Miss Foster, and she took me to meet Lincoln T. Hudson, the Vice President of Advertising for the Midwest. He explained the details about the position of Advertising Representative for *Ebony* that was being offered to me. After meeting with him I was directed to go back to see Miss Foster, who gave me the official offer of employment letter. The starting salary was significantly more than the offer from Skil.

In June 1972, I officially joined the staff of *Ebony* Magazine as the youngest Advertising Representative they had ever hired. Every day that I arrived for work, I was amazed by my surroundings. From the time, I entered the front of the building and passed through the revolving door, I felt special. It was impossible not to feel special entering the lobby of

Johnson Publishing Company. It was a grand two-story lobby tastefully filled with magnificent sculptures, artwork, rugs and a custom built red sectional sofa positioned next to an eighteen foot wall of bronze and Mozambique wood. When I stepped off the elevator on the floor that housed the Advertising Department, it was, as if I had arrived at a new destination. I was transformed and soothed by the softness of the beige, taupe, gold and tan that tastefully decorated the floor. Each floor in the building was designed to meet the functional requirements for the departments it housed as well as make a unique design statement.

The advertising department management consisted of Lincoln T. Hudson, VP of Advertising Sales; Ike Payne, Advertising Production Manager and Ben Hamilton, Sales Manager. The advertising sales team included me, Larry Hovell, Merv Harris, John Alexander, John Salter and later Dennis Boston. We each had an account list of existing and potential advertisers. Selling advertising space entailed researching and understanding the client's primary and secondary marketing targets, versus the buying habits of the readers of *Ebony* Magazine relative to the clients' product or service. That information would have to be assembled into a proposal for presentation to the client or the client's advertising agency. I was very good at doing the research and preparing proposals.

Lincoln Hudson was a former fighter pilot with the Tuskegee Airmen. He was a soft-spoken gentleman who used his likeable demeanor, combined with his determination and enthusiasm, to sell. Ben Hamilton was just the opposite of Mr. Hudson. He was like a bull in a china shop. If he couldn't guilt the client into a sale, he would muscle his way through the sell. Ike Payne, like Mr. Hudson, was soft spoken. He was thorough and knew how to apply pressure when necessary to get the ads in-house to meet closing dates.

Larry Hovell, who I called "Pusher Man", was tall and medium-complexioned with a nice grade of hair. I called him Pusher Man because he had a large Afro and reminded me of some of the Black characters in the Pam Grier/Foxy Brown and Ron O'Neal/Superfly movies. Also, he was known for enjoying a little weed. His mother was Ellen Stewart; she owned the off-off-Broadway theatre called LaMama in the East Village section of lower Manhattan in New York. He came out of the broadcast industry and at the time was married to one of the on-air radio personalities named Robin. Merv Harris was from the West Side of Chicago and had previously worked for Readers Digest before coming to Johnson Publishing Company (JPC). He was short, brown-skinned and a little on the heavy side. His claim to fame was that he was a strong closer and very likeable. John Alexander was the strong quiet type that fancied himself a ladies' man. He sold advertising space for the Midwest in *Jet* Magazine exclusively, and as a result I did not have much interaction with him. I do know that he seemed to always meet his weekly quotas for ad sales in *Jet*. John Salter was a tall and imposing guy who didn't stick around long enough for me to get to know him. He was replaced by Dennis Boston, who was also tall and imposing. He was about 6'4" and at least 250 pounds. Dennis came from the rental car industry and had previously worked for the Hertz Corporation before Mr. Johnson convinced him to come to JPC. He had a commanding voice and presence.

The challenge with selling advertising space in *Ebony* or *Jet* Magazine was that you first had to convince most advertisers of the importance of the Black consumer market. This was done in part based on the theory that although our numbers were smaller relative to the general market our consumption levels/indexes were higher and especially with big ticket items. Mr. Johnson commissioned a study done by one of the leading research firms – Yankolovich, to show that Blacks tended to over consume (relative to their incomes), certain durable goods like expensive cars,

123

appliances, stereo equipment and furniture, as well as luxury items such as jewelry and furs. The notion behind the theory was that since most Blacks were denied access to the American Dream, they compensated for it by purchasing things that gave the impression they had arrived. The final piece of the sale was that there was no other media outlet, Black or (White), that could deliver aspiring Blacks the way *Ebony* or *Jet* could. We also had to dispel the idea that major advertisers could effectively reach Blacks through their general market advertising initiatives. We told them advertising in *Ebony* and *Jet* was a sign of respect. It meant they valued the Black consumer market and the media outlets supported by it.

The Yankolovich research was rolled out in New York. We were all sent to the New York office that was managed by William P. Grayson. Bill Grayson was responsible for all sales on the east coast, and given the plethora of large companies and agencies in New York, his office generated top billings. When it came to advertising sales he was definitely "the man." Mr. Johnson appreciated and fully respected his talents. All of us, except John Alexander, flew out together on the same flight. We met at the airport and boarded our flight. We were flying first class, which was one of the benefits of working for Mr. Johnson. Everything around him and everything he did was always first class. Merv and Larry arrived at the airport together, and I noticed they were laughing and joking. As soon as we got seated Larry, who was seated behind Dennis and I on the aisle, asked Merv, who was seated one row in front of us on the aisle on the opposite side, to pass the bag. Merv pulled out of his carry-on bag a greasy brown bag with chicken wings and passed it across the aisle to Larry. Dennis and I could not believe they were going to eat those greasy chicken wings on the plane sitting in first class. Dennis immediately went into his mode of 'I don't see them, and I don't know them'. Larry realized what Dennis was doing and reached into the greasy bag and said, "Dennis here's a wing. You know you want one." Dennis continued to ignore him and just as Larry was about to toss a wing over the seat to Dennis, the stewardess arrived. She told Larry and Merv, they were making the other passengers uncomfortable and asked them to put the food away or hand it over. They put the wing bag away and remained quiet for the rest of the flight. As embarrassing as it was, it was also funny and I could not help but laugh throughout the entire flight. Every time I thought about what they did I would break out laughing.

The trip to New York and the Yankolovich research was great news. It provided credibility to what we had been saying to advertisers about the consumption levels of the Black consumer market. At the end of the week instead of returning to Chicago on Friday, we all agreed to stick around for the weekend. Larry had volunteered that we could stay with him at his mothers' place in the East Village. She lived in a large loft above the LaMama Theatre. Friday night we decided to hang out in the East Village and went to a local bar/eatery at the end of the block where the theatre was located. Everybody in the area seemed to know Larry and greeted him warmly. When we arrived at the bar several people came over to our table to say hello to Larry. During the course of the evening, a woman sitting at a table not far from us kept looking over at us. She was dressed to the nines and heavily made up. One member of our group, who shall remain nameless, commented that she was checking him out. Larry said, "Why don't you go over and buy her a drink. If you like I can introduce you." Larry made the introduction and came back to the table. Looking across at them, they seemed to be hitting it off while Larry kept grinning and laughing to himself. We kept asking Larry what was so funny, and finally he said to take a close look at her hands and feet. The moment he said that we knew she was not a woman. He said she was one of the neighborhood transvestites. I said somebody needs to tell him, and when we do he is going to kill you. Larry went over and got him, and as he was walking back to the table told him. He blew up and stormed out the bar threatening to kill Larry. We laughed about this for days and weeks to come.

Working for Johnson Publishing Company was not only a great adventure; it was also a huge learning experience. Unlike most of my fellow graduates that were working for Fortune 500 companies, I had direct access to the company founder and CEO. Every contact I had with Mr. Johnson, he was mindful of my presence, and took the opportunity to try to teach me something about business. It took me years to fully appreciate the value of the experience. What I can say today, having worked for several Fortune 100 companies, is that I have never worked for a company more professional or well run. In fact, it is the only company I have worked for where the only thing that really mattered was performance and loyalty. Performing at your best was more than just doing a good job: it was a source of personal and collective pride. Pride inspired by the example set by Mr. and Mrs. Johnson; pride in being a part of one of America's greatest success stories; pride in redefining what a Black-owned and operated company could be.

Mr. and Mrs. Johnson showed great generosity to their employees during times of need and triumph, and the only thing they asked in return was loyalty. They believed in possibility and defied limitations; if they had the will, they found the way. There was a never-ending sense of family, and if you were part of the family you felt protected. They taught us that being true to who you are and following your dreams was one of the keys to their success. Through them, we learned the lesson that being Black did not mean being less, it just meant you had to do more. They perfected the art of entertaining, ranging from royalty, heads of state, Hollywood A-list actors and actresses, corporate leaders and politicians to church organizations. Regardless of their station in life, the one thing, they all agreed on was that Mr. and Mrs. Johnson made them feel like royalty. They had indeed become de facto Black royalty.

126

One of my biggest regrets is that I did not stay at JPC. The decision to leave was a difficult one. After a year, I realized that despite the efforts to help me make the transition that something was missing. I was great at researching and preparing presentations. I understood marketing and knew how to position the readers of *Ebony* relative to the product or service offered by the company. What I was missing was salesmanship. For many people, salesmanship comes natural and for others it has to be learned or developed. I recognized what was missing and conveyed that to Mr. Johnson. He decided that I should go to New York and spend a couple of weeks working with Bill Grayson. He indicated that if anyone could teach me salesmanship it was Mr. Grayson. I spent two weeks in New York going on calls with him. What I learned is that he was always prepared. He was well informed about things going on in the client's company and industry. He searched all the major newspapers and magazines looking for information. He could speak extemporaneously about most things. It was great seeing him in action, and I learned a lot. I came away from that experience realizing that I needed formal training; the kind that many of my classmates were receiving from the Fortune 500 companies they were employed by. I left JPC to go work for the 3M Company, a Fortune 500 company.

#

I learned through this experience that if you believed and trusted in God nothing was impossible. No circumstance of birth or other limitation can stop you from realizing what God has in store for you if you trust and believe in Him. For me John H. Johnson was living proof of this. He gave meaning to the words to the song that says, "There is no secret what God can do for you. What He has done for others, He will do for you." He made achieving your dreams more than wishful thinking. He made it a real possibility.

127

Philippians 4: 13 says, "I can do all things through Him who strengthens me."

Matthew 19: 26 tells us: "And looking at them Jesus said to them, 'With people this is impossible, but with God all things are possible."

Johnson Publishing Company

John H. Johnson

Eunice Johnson

Bidding Farewell to Chi-town,
Heading for Cincinnati

Being an adult frequently means you have to sometimes make drastic changes in your life when necessary. After an unsuccessful marriage and working for JPC and 3M Company, I decided it was time for a major change in my life, including the possibility of a change in scenery. While staying at the YMCA I was talking with Al Lawrence, and he suggested that I sign up for a job fair he was attending in three weeks that was sponsored by a recruiting company out of New York. I thought it was too late, but he said to give it a try. The way this particular job fair worked was that you submit your resume to them, and they would circulate it to their participating clients/companies. If a client/company had an interest in talking with you based on what they saw on the resume, they would schedule an interview. Much to my surprise, several large companies, including Kodak and Ford Motor Company, expressed an interest in talking with me. I went to the job fair and met with both of them as well as a few other companies and also attended several seminars put on by the company sponsoring the job fair. The interview with Kodak did not go well because they were interested in me for their Printing Products' Division, which was huge, given all the training and experience, I received from 3M Company selling printing products. I am sure they could tell that I had no real interest in continuing to sell print products.

The interview with Ford was just the opposite; it went well. The prospect of working for a car company was exciting, especially since it did not include working as a dealership car salesman. After the initial interview, I was contacted by the recruiter to let me know they were interested and wanted to talk with me again. The next step in the process was for them to schedule an interview at their corporate office in Dearborn, Michigan.

130

Several weeks later they flew me to Dearborn for an interview. This was my first time experiencing what I later discovered was called a series of "round-robin" interviews where you meet with four-to-six managers for a half an hour each. The purpose of this was to allow them to look at you from different perspectives plus see how you handled the stress. I apparently did well because I received a callback from the corporate recruiter I met with during the interviews to let me know they were still interested. He indicated that he was going to send my paperwork over to several of the District Offices with openings for trainees, which was their entry level position, to see which one had an interest in talking with me. He called back after several weeks to let me know the Cincinnati District Office for the Lincoln-Mercury Division was interested in having me come in for an interview.

I knew very little about Cincinnati and had to get out a map to see exactly where it was located. I flew to Cincinnati and went through another series of round-robin interviews. My first impression of Cincinnati, beside it being very hilly, was that it was an interesting mixture of old and new. I could definitely tell that I was in the South; by the way, people looked and spoke, which caused me a little concern. During the course of the interviews, I learned that everyone started off working as a trainee. Typically, the first rotation was working in the Distribution Department, where you tracked the production of the vehicles ordered by the district from the initial order entry to the building and shipping of the vehicle to the dealership. The next rotation was working in either the Business or Retail Management Department. Business Management was responsible for reviewing the financial statements submitted by the dealers monthly for accuracy, trends and consistency. Retail Management handled the dealer placement process to make sure newly appointed dealers and existing dealers were properly located in the market to maximize sales. They also looked at different trends and patterns in each market the district was responsible for to determine the ideal location for dealerships both currently and in the future. After an exhausting day of interviewing, I flew back to Chicago. A couple of weeks passed, and I finally heard back that they wanted to make me an offer.

In May 1975, I packed up what few things I had and moved to Cincinnati, Ohio. Before leaving, I discovered talking with my mother that she had a cousin, Lilly Brown, who lived in Cincinnati. I also learned through my brother that Bill Adkins (one of his childhood friends) lived in Dayton, Ohio and worked for General Motors. Lilly was married to Mr. Earl, a minister at a small church in the "Over the Hill" area of Cincinnati. She had two children, Shirley and Andrew Wallace, and was raising Andrew's two sons. Andrew was in prison for felony murder. Shirley was a teenager going through a boy-hungry phase, in love with a curly haired Creole-looking guy named Steve Haynes. He was bad news from start to finish. Bill Adkins, who at one point in time was on the same path as my brother, had turned his life around and was a District Service Manager for the Pontiac Division of General Motors. Having been in the automobile industry for a while, he was very instrumental in helping me make the transition into the industry. Whenever I had questions or needed advice, Bill was a just a phone call away. Since where he lived in Dayton was only 40 minutes away, we could easily meet for dinner or drinks.

After meeting with my newly discovered relatives and Bill Adkins, I got busy looking for a place to stay. Cincinnati was known as the city built on seven hills. While there is a lot of confusion about what the seven hills are; most would agree they include Mt. Adams, Mt. Auburn, Mt. Lookout, Walnut Hills, Clifton Heights, Vine Street Hill and Price Hill. The one area I was most attracted to was Mt. Adams near downtown. However, I ultimately decided I wanted to live on the north end of town where the office was located. I moved to the Montgomery area. They were building a lot of new apartment complexes on Montgomery Road near I-275. One of the complexes called Harper's Point seemed to have it all: a great clubhouse, fabulous pools, ample tennis courts, fitness center, luscious landscaping and beautiful townhouses. I leased a one-bedroom upper unit with a cathedral ceiling.

My first rotation at work was in the Distribution Department. The Department Manager at the time was Bob. He was from the Virginia area and was going through rotation at the department manager level. Shirley was the Domestic Distribution Manager responsible for all domestically produced vehicles and Chuck was the Import Car Distribution Manager that took care of all the imports. I was the Scheduling Clerk, and my job was to schedule each dealer's fair share of the daily production at the various manufacturing plants based on orders in house. It was also my job to make sure dealers submitted their orders in line with the monthly wholesale agreement they signed. This could be challenging because oftentimes dealers would sign the wholesale agreement to purchase a certain number and type of vehicles just to get their Zone Manager off their back. Others would sign the agreement based on a sales projection that was more wishful thinking than on reality. To avoid building excess inventory many dealers would delay or not submit their orders. It didn't take me long to get the hang of the job. My biggest problem was winning the hearts and minds of Shirley, Chuck and the dealers. The previous trainee was a guy named Rick Vonderhaar, who was now the Zone Manager for Louisville. Rick was at least 6'4" or 6'5" and a former college basketball player for the University of North Carolina. Shirley loved basketball and was a Tar Heel fan and very proud of it. Rick did a good job and was very likeable. Everything I did was compared to the way he did it.

The social scene in Cincinnati was very interesting. Unlike Chicago, there were only a few clubs, White or Black. The one club frequented by most Blacks–the Viking, was what folks from Chicago would call a hole-in-the-wall. There was nothing upscale at all about the club. It was hot and sweaty because it did not have air conditioning. I would go there occasionally, and it was obvious to most of the girls I met that I was not from Cincinnati. They would quickly ask me "where are you from?", and say, "I could tell you were not from Cincinnati because you talk different and dress too nice to be from here." Most people I met from Cincinnati were laid back and lackadaisical about most things. They were not very ambitious and happy to have what little they had. I, on the other hand, always wanted more and was unapologetic about it.

After six months in the Distribution Department, I finally won the hearts and minds of my colleagues and the dealers. I was moved to the Business Management Department where I spent five months analyzing the financial statements submitted by the dealers. There was a rumor going around that a zone was going to become available in the next couple of months because one of our Department Managers was being considered for a position at headquarters in Dearborn. This could result in one of our Zone Managers getting promoted to come inside as a Department Manager. This would leave a zone open, and I was next in line to go into the field. Normally, what would happen is that one of the Zone Managers in a B zone would be promoted to an A zone. The B zones covered the rural areas in our District Office, and the A zones included the metropolitan areas in the district like Cincinnati, Dayton and Columbus Ohio; Louisville and Lexington Kentucky and Indianapolis, Indiana. The rumor turned out to be true, and they shuffled the deck and I ended up being assigned the Southern Indiana zone. My zone covered everything south of Indianapolis. It included cities in Indiana like Shelbyville, Bloomington, Linton, Jasper, Terre Haute and Evansville. I was assigned my first field car and was off and running.

It was ironic that my promotion came at the same time I was beginning to feel a lot more comfortable living in Cincinnati. I had met and made friends with Charles and Sharon Porter, a couple born and raised in Cincinnati that lived next door to me. Charles worked for Xerox and Sharon

134

was employed as a Claims Adjuster for Allstate. Through them, I was slowly being introduced into the Black bourgeoisie of Cincinnati. One of Sharon's older brothers, Steve Reece Sr., was actively involved in the community and politics in Cincinnati. I had also started dating again. In fact, I was dating several girls. One of the girls I dated was Roslyn. She was older and came from a large prominent Black family in Cincinnati. Roslyn was very serious and looking for a prospective husband, which she thought she had found in me. She had older brothers, who were very successful and was looking for someone who would meet their approval. One bad habit she had was what I called marking her territory. Whenever she would come by, she secretly made sure she left something personal behind so that any other female visitors would know I was dating someone else. Most times when she came by my apartment, she would make dinner, which frequently included potato salad (her favorite not mine). The standing joke among my friends and other visitors who happened to go into my refrigerator was "I see the potato salad lady has been here." They knew that while I could cook a few things, that potato salad was not one of them. During the time, I was dating Roslyn; I was also dating a girl named Roxslyn, who was just the opposite. I nicknamed her Foxie Roxie. She was younger and a complete free spirit. The only thing they had in common was that they were both buxom. All she was looking for was to have fun. She loved going out and traveling.

Being a Zone Manager meant I had less time for socializing, since the job required you to be out traveling calling on your dealers. Most weeks I would leave on a Monday morning and not return to Cincinnati until Friday afternoon, unless for some other reason I had to be in town for meetings. I loved the freedom of being on the road calling on dealers. I felt empowered and also appreciated the opportunity to learn a different side of the car business counseling the dealers. If your dealers liked you, they took great pride in seeing you be successful and would do everything they could to help you. About fifteen months later I was moved to an A zone, Louisville, Kentucky. On one hand, it was a great zone to have because it included the district's largest dealer, Herb Vine, who owned a dealership called Bluegrass Lincoln-Mercury. The downside of the zone was that it included places in parts of eastern Kentucky such as London, Somerset, Harlan, Hazard, Neon and Bristol, Virginia. The kind of places where the people who lived there didn't take to kindly to strangers and especially ones that did not look anything like them. To get to my dealers located east of I-75, I had to drive through coal mining towns where I knew there were no hotels I could stay the night in. It meant when I called on those dealers I had to start very early and would not have time for lunch or a lot of chit chatting. The goal was to call on the dealers and make sure I got to either Bristol, Virginia when heading east, or Somerset, Kentucky off I-75 before nightfall when I was traveling west. I knew that when I got to either of these locations, I could find a hotel that I would be comfortable staying in.

I was doing relatively well in my job and felt fairly secure until we got a new General Sales Manager, Bernie Finan. We reported to him and he reported to Mr. Ramsey, the District Manager. Bernie came over from the Ford side of the house. He came in making changes, which rubbed most of the guys (including me) the wrong way. He loved calling me "bro" which I hated and thought was unprofessional. Bernie, who was White, played college basketball with a lot of Blacks and was comfortable bantering back and forth having spent time with them in the locker room. Somehow he thought it was okay to treat me the same way, except, I did not respond in kind. He thought I had an attitude, which set the tone of our relationship.

We were also going through a difficult wholesale period as a result of the fallout from the gas embargo of the early '70s. People were no longer buying big cars, especially luxury ones, because they could no longer afford the gas prices. The demand for small cars went through the roof and the problem for us was we had very few to sell. This brought with it intense pressure to try to wholesale the big stuff, which the dealers were resisting taking because that's not what their customers wanted. Most of my dealers were focusing on selling used cars to survive waiting for us to start producing small cars they could sell. It got to the point that we spent most days in the office locked in the conference room, calling our dealers trying to convince them to take cars the district had ordered because they refused to order them. It is called "sales bank" when cars are ordered this way. The normal sales process is that you wholesale vehicles to your dealers, which means you get them to agree to a certain number of units of production on a monthly basis. After the wholesale is complete the dealer is required to submit their orders during a certain time period in line with their wholesale commitment. When the market goes south two things happen: dealers refuse to sign their wholesale agreement, or refuse to submit the orders needed to produce the vehicles they committed to in their wholesale order. Contrary to what most auto manufacturers say publicly, they order the vehicles to keep production going with the hopes, they can sell them to the dealers after they're built, which historically has created even bigger problems.

Having spent my first two years in Cincinnati in hot pursuit of female companionship, I was reaching a point where I was beginning to tire of the chase. Bill Adkins, who I spent time with on a regular basis, had met a young lady named Allean Brown through someone in his office. She had been introduced to him as someone he might want to date. The person who made the introduction was unaware that he was dating someone else. Bill thought Allean, who lived in Cincinnati, was a nice young lady I might be interested in getting to know. One evening he had me meet him at a club in Cincinnati called the Vault and unbeknownst to me, he had invited her to join us. He knew that I would not agree to a blind date and thought this was the best way to introduce us. He also knew that if I was interested

137

I would take it from there and if not there would be no pressure on either side. She was tall and medium complexion with huge dimples. What I found most interesting about her was that she was not from Cincinnati and appeared to be well educated and cultured. She was from Cleveland, Ohio and had a bachelor's degree in Fine Arts from the University of Indiana and had spent the past couple of years attending the University of Cincinnati working on a degree in architecture. At the time we met, she had taken a hiatus from working on her degree because of some problems she was having with the department chairman. She was working for a company called Fotomat overseeing site selection and putting up Fotomat kiosks around the city.

Allean was bright, engaging and a great conversationalist. She seemed to be a wealth of knowledge about most things, whether it was technical, cultural or political. It was clear that she was well read and came from a good background. Her mother, Ozella was a schoolteacher and her father, J. Harold Brown, had a Master's degree in music. He was involved with the Cleveland Orchestra, Karamu House and the Cleveland Playhouse as well as countless other arts related organizations in Cleveland. I was fascinated by her knowledge and what appeared to be her southern charm and hospitality, which she lavished on me. She was also a very nice person and appeared to be very independent. She could build anything, and did a great job making many of her clothes. Most people thought we were a perfect match. After dating for a few months we decided to live together. Allean was renting a big old house in a trendy area near the University of Cincinnati. Combining forces was going to be interesting. I liked places that were modern with sleek clean lines, and she preferred living spaces that were big and old. We spent a lot time looking at places in Mt. Adams and other areas that had a lot of newly renovated apartments. I thought this was the perfect compromise. Most of the apartments were large units in older buildings; the interiors were completely renovated to give the units a

138

modern and sleek urban feel. After looking at dozens of units like this, which she kept saying were too sterile, we ended up taking an upper unit in a large house.

The house was located in Mt. Auburn, a historically designated district with unique houses of Federal, Greek Revival, Italian Villa, Romanesque Revival and Georgian Revival styles. The house we moved into looked like a Swiss chalet. Unfortunately, it was the only notable house on our street. The rest of the houses were older single- and multiple-family homes and a few apartment buildings, most in need of repair. The house had been partially renovated, primarily the first floor apartment occupied by the building owner and the common area. Our unit had been converted into a bi-level unit by adding stairs off the dining room to take you to the upper level, which was previously a large attic space. The door to our unit was on the second floor, and led into the living room that had a wood-burning fireplace. The kitchen, which had not been renovated, was on the same level to the right of the living room. If you continued turning left after walking through the living room you ended up in the dining room with the steps that led to the second floor of the unit. The upper level had a large wide-open room which we used as a recreation area and work room. It also had a bedroom, bathroom and a large closet. Unlike the units in Mt. Adams none of the fixtures or appliances were new; the floors had not been recently sanded and the kitchen cabinets, sink, countertops and appliances were not new. This was far from being a perfect compromise. It was a step back no matter how much I wanted to think otherwise.

Although I was disappointed with our living accommodations, I tried to make the best of it. I was still convinced that things would work out, because like everybody else, I thought we were a perfect match. In June 1977, after living together for a while, we decided to make it official and get married. The big question was when and where. We decided to get married in Los Angeles at Christmas. My brother lived in California and so did both of Allean's sisters (Thelma and Althea). My family already had plans to spend Christmas in California at my brother's house in Palos Verdes, California. Bill Adkins, who I wanted to be my best man, typically spent Christmas in California, where he lived before being transferred to Dayton. So all we needed to do was get her parents and her cousin Val, who she planned on having as one of her bridesmaids to Los Angeles. We got married on December 26, 1977 at The Wayfarers Chapel in Palos Verdes, California. The church was designed by Lloyd Wright, the son of Frank Lloyd Wright, and was also known as the "Glass Church." We later had a reception in Cleveland, Ohio for friends and family that could not make it to LA, including my co-workers from Lincoln-Mercury.

A few months after getting married the situation at work got a lot worse. My relationship with Bernie Finan deteriorated to the point we could barely stand being in the same room with each other. The wholesale situation had become so severe that we spent most of our time in the office selling sales bank. I became so overwhelmed by the wholesale effort and constantly being attacked by Bernie that I quit without having another job lined up. This was a scary situation to be in as a newlywed. Much to my surprise, Allean, who had quit her job at Fotomat before we got married and was now working for a roofing company, was very supportive. Being at home everyday made me keenly aware of all of Allean's unfinished projects: from not completing the requirements for her degree in architecture to things around the house she started but did not finish, and all sorts of sewing and art projects. I was beginning to discover that she was full of ideas, which she was quick to initiate but slow to complete. Unlike Allean, I had a more driven personality and took great pride in always finishing what I started. I was uncomfortable surrounded by tons of unfinished projects. I took it upon myself to help her by completing as many of the unfinished projects as I could. This included learning how to sew in an effort to help her complete many of her unfinished sewing projects.

140

Much to my surprise I was pretty good at it and discovered my creative side, which heretofore I had not fully explored. In fact, we started a business in our home designing and sewing clothing for professional women, which was of course another one of her ideas.

My job search landed me a position as a Sales Rep with Anchor Hocking, a glass company in Lancaster, Ohio. I spent several months in a small studio apartment I rented in Lancaster, while I was going through training and waiting to be assigned a territory. I was eventually assigned a territory in Philadelphia working out of the office located in Bala Cynwyd, a suburb of Philadelphia. Once again, I rented a small apartment while we looked for permanent housing and Allean looked for a job. Allean was familiar with Philadelphia because she previously lived there during one of her internships as part of the architecture program. After being in Philadelphia for three or four months and still living in temporary quarters, I got a call from a recruiter for Volkswagen of America (VWOA). They had just recently repurchased the distribution rights back from one of their distributors and were in the process of expanding the regional office in Columbus, Ohio to take over responsibility for the dealer network previously managed by the distributor. They were in the process of hiring five or six new District Sales Managers to call on the dealers. A VWOA District Sales Manager was the equivalent of a Lincoln Mercury Zone Manager. I interviewed for one of the positions and was selected to become the District Sales Manager for the Detroit District. After spending several months in Columbus learning the Volkswagen systems I was off to Detroit.

#

Leaving Cincinnati and moving to Detroit was filled with uncertainty as we embarked upon creating a new life for ourselves. It was a chance to get back into the automobile industry, which I had discovered that I truly enjoyed and missed. For Allean, it was an opportunity to finish her degree and pursue her career in architecture. And for us it was a second chance to find a home that reflected both of us. We left Cincinnati filled with hopes and plans to find happiness. We prayed and believed that everything would work out and be okay.

Jeremiah 29: 11-14 says, "For I know the plans I have for you," declares the LORD, "plans to prosper you and not to harm you, plans to give you hope and a future. Then you will call upon Me and come and pray to Me, and I will listen to you. You will seek Me and find Me when you seek Me with all your heart. I will be found by you," declares the LORD, "and will bring you back from captivity."

Downtown Cincinnati from Covington, Kentucky

Harper's Point

Next Stop, Motown

I had mixed feeling about moving to Detroit. I was definitely ready to leave Cincinnati, which I felt I had outgrown some time ago. However, the thought of going to Detroit created some concern for me. In 1979 Detroit was a city divided along racial, social and economic lines. As the automobile capital of the world it was a one-industry town and as the industry went so did the fortunes of Detroit. Coleman A. Young, Detroit's mayor since 1973, was a polarizing force. He was Detroit's first Black mayor and for most Blacks, he represented the first real opportunity for Blacks to achieve political power. It was clear that Blacks ran the local government in the city. However, the economic power remained firmly in the hands of Whites and in particular, the automotive power brokers. Whites viewed Coleman Young as obstinate and a threat to their way of life. As a result many made a fast exit to the surrounding suburbs leaving Detroit, predominantly Black and without a strong tax base. The population in Detroit went from a high of 1.8 million in the '50s to less than half of that in the '70s.

The first thing we needed to do was select an area where we wanted to live. I spent time traveling to Detroit while I worked for Lincoln-Mercury and was more interested in looking for new housing in an area like Southfield. I had several friends who lived in Southfield. Allean on the other hand, was more interested in looking at older homes in neighborhoods like Boston-Edison and Indian Village. Both were historic districts. Since I would be working out of my home calling on dealers in Detroit and the surrounding suburban communities, and towns as far west as Adrian, Michigan it didn't really matter where we lived. Once again, I acquiesced and agreed to focus our search in the Boston-Edison area.

Boston-Edison was located west of downtown Detroit near Grand Boulevard where General Motors' headquarters was located. The neighborhood consisted of over 900 homes, primarily built from 1905-1925, which made it the largest residential historic district in the nation. Most of the homes were large with anywhere from 12 to 20 rooms and included architectural features like large foyers, hardwood floors, multiple wood burning fireplaces, wainscoting and crown molding, Pewabic tile and marble and leaded glass doors and windows to name a few. Some of the historically significant residents were Henry Ford, James Couzens, Horace Rackham, Charles T. Fisher, Peter E. Martin, C. Harold Wills, Clarence W. Avery, Sebastian S. Kresge, and Clarence Burton. In more recent times during the '60s it was home to Berry Gordy, the founder of Motown. The downside of too many of the homes was that over the years many of them had fallen into a state of ill repair and needed a lot of work. The other problem was they were surrounded by neighborhoods on all four sides in various states of decline experiencing urban blight. All Allean could see was the architectural significance of the housing and the opportunity for us to get in on the ground floor. Her fear was that before long the area would be overrun with young White kids with fists full of dollars renovating everything in sight. She thought it was the perfect place for us.

We started looking for homes and quickly discovered one that was owned by two gay guys, Norm and Dale, located on Chicago Blvd. The house had been completely renovated with brand new appliances and fixtures throughout; newly stained trim and moldings and refinished hardwood floors. It had been tastefully painted and decorated, from top to bottom, both inside and outside. As much as I resisted the idea of living in Boston-Edison, the house on Chicago was perfect, and I was excited. She could have her big old house with all of its architectural significance, and I could have the modern aspects that were important to me. My excitement soon ended when I discovered it was not shared by Allean. She agreed

145

that it was the perfect house for us but her hesitation was that it had not been done by us. You see, for Allean it was as much about doing as it was about having.

It took me a while to get over the news flash, that "we" should be renovating our own home and not looking for ones that were already renovated. I was clearly not prepared for this latest revelation, inasmuch as I had no interest in embarking upon a back-breaking, all consuming project of renovating a house, and especially one we would have to live in during the process. I am a creature of habit, and having order around me is extremely important. I don't function well in chaos and confusion. For the third time, I compromised and agreed to explore homes in the Boston-Edison area that we could renovate. We found a home located at 1956 West Boston Blvd that she thought had great potential. It was a three-story colonial that had 15 rooms with architectural features characteristic of the neighborhood and a two-car garage. The house was owned by Mrs. Jones, who lived there by herself. She was recently divorced and it was obvious she could not afford to maintain or do the needed repairs on the house. The house had urine stained and soiled carpet throughout most of the rooms on the first and second floor. Many of the rooms were painted hideous colors like blood red and deep blue. There were signs of leaks all around the house and the roof was in questionable condition. The front porch of the house was a semi-circular shape and had four tall columns that supported a decorative upper balcony with wood railings. Most of the railing was rotted, and the small roof area leaked. The plumbing worked, for the most part, but it was obvious that repairs were needed. The electrical was a combination of circuit breakers and the old knob and tube wiring. The most immediate concern was the furnace; it was a steam-heated furnace with a huge crack in it. You had to be careful when putting water into the furnace not to fill it up beyond the level where the crack was located. If you did, the furnace would go out. When this happened you would have to wait hours without heat for the furnace to dry out before you could turn it back on. In spite of all of this we made an offer on the house. We purchased it for $50,000 on a land-contract with a three-year balloon payment. because no bank would provide a mortgage on a house in this condition. It would not pass one single inspection even in Detroit.

The new job was going well. I liked most of my dealers and had begun to build a good working relationship with them, which was essential to being successful in Detroit. Going into the job I was told that it was important to build a good relationship with the dealers so that when they had problems, they would come to us and not go to Corporate. Our Corporate offices were in the process of relocating from Englewood Cliffs, New Jersey to Troy, Michigan, and it was a big concern that the dealers would inundate them with their issues instead of working through us. Dealers going to their Corporate office was the norm in Detroit, because that's where all the Corporate offices for the Big 3 were located. My management had heard all the horror stories of things that happened with the other manufacturers and wanted to avoid it happening with us. Therefore, my relationship with my dealers was seen as crucial. As for Allean, it took a while, but she finally landed a position with Bechtel Corporation, which at the time was one of the world's largest engineering, construction, management and development services firms. Bechtel is the 5th largest privately-owned firm in the U.S. She worked out of their office in Ann Arbor bringing online the Fermi Nuclear Power Plant in Monroe, Michigan.

The house we purchased on Boston Blvd. was located between 12th and 14th streets, and at the time we only had one vacant house on our street. Most of the houses on our street were fairly well maintained by other working professionals. A couple of the families on the block had been there since the late '50s and early '60s. The house to the west of us was owned by Mrs. Binion. She was recently widowed when we moved in and was living in the home by herself. She had grown children, including a married daughter and a son, who was a physician that graduated from Morehouse College. Her family owned a medical supply business. To the east of us was the infamous Rev. Otis. He lived in the house with Liz and her two sons and Liz's grandmother. Liz was barely 18 or 19 years old. Rev. Otis, who was in his early forties drove a long black Cadillac limousine and was the pastor of a church not far from where we lived. His Sunday Service was broadcast live every Sunday, and he could be heard challenging listeners to try God. He would say, "I double-dawg dare you" or he would offer up a three or four-digit number that most of his listeners used to play the lottery. We later found out that Rev. Otis had a wife and another family that lived in one of the much larger and nicer homes on Ponchartrain Blvd. near Palmer Woods. He and his wife were going through a separation/divorce, and he had been removed from a much larger church where he had been the pastor. This happened when they found out about the separate life he was living with Liz and the two children he had fathered with her.

Directly across the street from us lived Warren and Jeannie Smith. Warren was an engineer working for Turner Construction and Jeannie managed all of their rental properties. They owned anywhere from 15-20 different pieces of property, ranging in size from single family homes and two- to four-family rental units to a large apartment complex with 40 or 50 units. They would buy the property for taxes or some other ridiculously low price and do all the repairs themselves. Warren could fix or repair anything and owned every tool known to man. Next door to the Smiths was the George and Carman N'Namdi family. George owned an art gallery in Detroit called the G.R. N'Namdi Gallery, and Carman was the Founder and CEO of Nataki Talibah Schoolhouse of Detroit. They lived an Afrocentric lifestyle and had three or four kids. Also on the block was the Barthwell Family. Sidney Barthwell, Sr. was in retirement and had sold off most of the

148

drugstores he previously owned. Besides Mr. and Mrs. Barthwell, their son Sidney Barthwell Jr. lived in the house. Sidney Jr., whose life had somehow gotten derailed in the '60s with drugs and politics, seemed to be stuck there. He was going through a process of trying to get his life back on track, which he eventually did. He went back to undergraduate school at Wayne State University and finished his degree. He applied to and was accepted into law school at Harvard University where he received a degree in law. After practicing law in Detroit for a while, he became a judge.

Work on the house, which began in earnest, after we moved in, started to slow down after Allean went to work for Bechtel. One of the first things we did was to remove the stained and soiled carpets on the first floor and have the hardwood floors refinished. This made a huge difference in making that part of the house feel less disgusting. The next project we took on was stripping the paint from the leaded bevel glass doors and windows in the front foyer. This was my first experience with stripping paint, and I had no idea how laborious, tedious, and messy it could be. I discovered during the process that a lot of the wood used for the wainscoting did not match, which meant it was never intended to be stripped and stained. I ended up stripping the doors and windows and painting the rest of the trim, molding and wainscoting in the foyer as well as adding bamboo wallpaper that matched the paint. The next step was to tackle the rest of the hallway with the front staircase you entered after the foyer. Doing this was fairly simple because all it involved was painting and wallpapering the hallway, which led to the living room, dining room, breakfast nook and pantry/kitchen. Completing the hallway required removing and repairing the staircase railing. There were several rails missing that had to be custom made, and removing the railing was the only way to properly sand and refinish the steps. The staircase went from the first floor to a landing with a huge leaded glass picture window and window seat. To get to the second floor you had to make a sharp left turn on the landing and take four or five additional steps.

A couple of noteworthy points need to be made here. First a lot of the work I described here I did because Allean was tied up with her new job. Her commute time to Ann Arbor was 45 minutes each way, and she often had to work overtime or was away for training.

As much as we preferred working on the cosmetic aspects of the renovation, we could not continue to ignore the structural things that needed to be done. We hired a roofer to patch most of the leaks on the roof, and then we turned our attention to the leaking furnace. We ordered a new furnace, which our neighbor Warren had agreed to help install. He had installed several furnaces in buildings they owned. The week before the furnace was scheduled to be delivered; I was in Columbus, Ohio attending meetings. When I arrived back in Detroit Friday afternoon, I knew I had to get busy tearing down the old cast iron furnace so the new one could be delivered and Warren could help install it. I spent Friday afternoon/evening and all day Saturday wielding a twenty-pound sledgehammer at the furnace trying to break it up into small enough pieces that could be carried out of the basement. I got it done, and true to his word Warren helped install the new furnace. I was so sore and fatigued that I ended up sick for a week and had to stay in bed.

From an outside perspective, it looked as if "we" were making progress on the house. However, I knew that it was not "us" making progress; it was "me." Having a driven personality would not allow me to start something and not finish it; besides, having a sense of order and comfortable surroundings was, and is, extremely important to me. I spent every waking moment that I was not working for Volkswagen, working on the house. Fortunately for me, not only was my hard work around the house paying off, so were my efforts calling on the dealers. I was promoted to a position at headquarters in Troy responsible for advertising production. In my new job, it was my responsibility to oversee advertising production done by our ad agency, to make sure we did no go over budget. The new job required being in the office daily other than when I was meeting with the agency in New York; in LA or New York working out the details with one of the production companies we used or on-site filming a TV commercial. The new job was great, except that it left me very little freedom to work on renovating the house other than on the weekend or when I took off.

Renovating a house not only puts a strain on you physically and financially; it also puts a strain on your relationship. Even at a slower pace, I continued to make progress going from room to room. After finishing the foyer/hallway I started on the living room; I then went to the dining room and the kitchen. In the living room, we painted the walls a cream color, put up gold mini-blinds on the windows and made swag curtains. Then we painted a plum accent color on the crown molding and painted the fireplace black lacquer with gold accents on the floral design carved into the mantel. We finished off the hearth with gold tiles. This gave the room a warm feeling with a dramatic look. In the dining room, we painted the wainscoting and trim a light cobalt blue color and put up a fabric with a large floral print on the upper portion of the wall. In the kitchen, we painted the walls a rattan beige color and used white automobile pinstripes to create a square geometric pattern on the walls. We stripped and stained the kitchen cabinets except for the inset, which we covered in a beige fabric with white diagonal diamond shaped lines on it. For the countertops Allean came up with the idea from something she had seen in a magazine. We tore up brown paper bags into small and medium size pieces and then glued them on the countertop until it was all covered, which created a marble like effect. Once this was done we used a polyurethane epoxy and resin to seal and protect the counter tops. It gave the tops a high gloss finish and protected the surface from damage.

Every year in Boston-Edison around Christmas time, they would have their annual Christmas home tour. The Christmas Walk involved soliciting five or six homeowners to open up their homes to be on the tour. They would advertise the event, which attracted several hundred people each year that purchased tickets to tour the homes. If you agreed to open up your home for the tour, part of your duties included escorting the different groups through your home, explaining the history of the house and all the things you've done to renovate it. We decided to put our house on the 1982 tour, which, by the way, was the same year I got promoted to the Manager of Special Events responsible for all Volkswagen, Porsche and Audi Shows and Exhibits. We put the house on the tour to give ourselves a timeframe for getting most of the renovation completed, in spite of the fact I was traveling a lot more with my new job. It was a lot of hard work on weekends, but we met our goal and everybody oohed and aahed about how beautiful the house was. It was 95 percent completed and in my mind it was time to sit back and enjoy the fruits of our labor. I figured I could work on completing the remaining 5 percent at my leisure. Allean, who by this time was having problems on her job at Bechtel, thought we should be buying and renovating properties like our neighbors the Smiths were doing. Again, I went along with her idea because I knew in my heart it would not be long before she was going to lose her job, which in fact, did happen. The condition upon which I agreed was that "she" and not "I" would have to oversee the renovation. My job was to help secure the property at the lowest possible cost and find funding to do the renovations. Over the next couple of years, we purchased three two-family units and a large complex with six row houses. I was able to buy the properties for the delinquent taxes or negotiate great deals with the owners. I was also able to secure a line of credit, so we could do the repairs. I had done my part and unfortunately Allean did not hold up her end of the bargain. In fairness, I must admit some of it was due in part to her being pregnant the summer of 1983.

As usual, I took on the projects myself and one by one was able to get the two-family units renovated and rented out. Renovating the row houses, which were located in the culture center area not far from Wayne State University, was going to require a lot more money and effort. By the time our blessed daughter Alyssa was born in March 1984, renovations on two of the three two-family units were completed and the units rented out.

By the way, when Alyssa was born, I barely made it back in time from Denver. As new parents we found we had very little energy or time to do anything, other than take care of Alyssa. However, we did find time to finish off the third two-family unit. The next year after Alyssa arrived, who was the love of my life, our circumstances and personal relationship really began to change. My mother, who was diabetic and still living in Chicago, was told that she had renal failure and was going to require kidney dialysis treatments. I was afraid to have her start the treatments living alone. My younger brother, Tyrone who had been living with her, had recently moved to Texas. We all agreed that she did not need to be alone and gave her the option of who she wanted to live with. She decided she wanted to move to Detroit to live with us.

Over the next three years instead of Allean and me becoming closer, we drifted farther and farther away from each other. My frustration level was growing daily. In spite of all the hard work that had gone into renovating the house we seemed to be in a constant state of disarray. Things were all over the house, and I felt like the walls were closing in on me. My frustration spilled over into my job and I ended up quitting my job in 1986. Allean was working for a minority-owned metal fabricating company preparing engineering drawings and specifications. It was clear that our relationship was in trouble. I felt unappreciated, and that all the compromises I had made throughout the relationship were for nothing. I was so busy being her knight in shining armor that I lost sight of my dreams. All of this manifested itself into resentment toward her, which was

153

growing steadily. I went from frustration to resentment and from resentment to anger, which signaled the end of our relationship. We went through a very messy separation, which led to a very nasty divorce.

The one bright spot was finding a new job and reconnecting with someone from my past. In January 1988, I started a new job as Vice President of Sales and Marketing, working for a minority-owned trucking company called Jones Transfer. The company was based out of Monroe, Michigan. The CEO, Gary White was one of my neighbors from Boston-Edison. He had taken an early retirement from Ford where he worked in Procurement and Supply. He wanted me to head up their Sales and Marketing operation and help him take the company to the next level. He already had a contract with Ford and wanted to expand into GM and Chrysler.

Also, that same year while attending the funeral for Derrick's mom, Bernice Agins, in Chicago, I ran into Rita Sutton. If you recall, Rita was the young lady I dated in high school and took to my senior prom. She was a nurse working at Michael Reese Hospital in the emergency room. I had not kept close track of her since high school but knew from my mother that she worked at the hospital. It seemed that every time I came home to Chicago or spoke with my mother by phone, she would say – "guess who I saw"? She would then proceed to tell me that she saw Rita and how great she looked. Whenever my mother went to the hospital to see one of her doctors, she made a point of stopping by the emergency room to say hi to Rita. It was no secret to me or anyone else that Rita was her favorite. At that moment in spite of everything else that was going on it seemed the right moment to reconnect. I didn't have to explain to her who I was or where I came from and most importantly she didn't want or need anything other than me. In the spring of 1988 my younger brother Tyrone returned to Chicago from Dallas, Texas. I knew he was gay but what I didn't know was that he had AIDS. Rita helped me try to take care of him and get him the

154

medical attention he needed. He finally succumbed to his illness and died in August of that year. A couple of months later Rita moved to Detroit.

#

At this stage of my life, a big part of it was about continued change and sacrifice. While I was growing comfortable with change and in many ways delighting in it, sacrifice was a difficult lesson to learn because I expected it to be equal and reciprocated as well as fully appreciated. What I discovered is that a lot of times it is neither.

What I had not learned is that sacrifice is based on what you value. It's not a sacrifice to give up something that you don't value for something you value more, it's a trade-off. In any meaningful relationship, you need to determine what each partner values and then identify the things that can potentially get in the way of each party achieving what they value. The sacrifice is the willingness to let go of those things that interfere for the good of the relationship, no matter how important they are to you. Because of the inevitable challenges, you will be faced with, in the end you have to decide whether you are willing to walk the walk, or just talk the talk.

Detroit skyline in the '70s

Detroit landmark – Fist

Spirit of Detroit statue

J. L. Hudson Building

1956 W. Boston

Row houses purchased to renovate

Alyssa age 2

Tyrone Jackson

CHAPTER 4

WORKING FOR CHRYSLER –
THE RIDE OF MY LIFE

Rebuilding Chrysler
Outside of North America

In March 1989, I was contacted by Mary Lou Joswick, an old friend who worked with me as a District Manager at Volkswagen. She was now working for Chrysler Corporation responsible for Sales Planning. After getting caught up, she wanted to know if I would be interested in talking with a representative from Chrysler's International Operations group. They were looking for someone with a strong automotive background in Marketing for a position as the Merchandising Manager. They specifically wanted someone knowledgeable about producing collateral materials and experienced with Shows and Exhibits and Special Events. She had discussed my background with HR, and they wanted to talk with me. I said sure, why not. I was contacted by HR and met with them. After establishing that my background and credentials were in order, and that I was a good fit for the position, they arranged for me to meet with someone from International.

Before the meeting, I learned that Chrysler was in the process of expanding the International group they inherited with the purchase of American Motors Corporation (AMC) and the Jeep Brand in 1987. This was being done in conjunction with plans to re-enter the International market after being gone for almost twelve years. In 1977 Chrysler closed its European Operations, and the following year sold Simca to Peugeot. Several of the Simca models found their way into the U.S. market in the form of the Dodge Omni and Plymouth Horizon. The sell-off of Chrysler's European operations was a precursor to the 1979 bailout Chrysler needed from the U.S. Government. Under the direction of Lee Iacocca, Chrysler, faced with the risk of going bankrupt, petitioned the federal government for loan guarantees to cover the $1.5 billion in private loans they were trying to secure. The government required Chrysler to find $2 billion in commitments or concessions (primarily from employee unions, backers and dealers) before they would act to guarantee the private loans. In response to Chrysler meeting the requirements, Congress passed the Chrysler Corporation Loan Guarantee Act of 1979, which was repaid in full in 1983.

During the meeting with International, I met with Tom Draur, who headed up Advertising for the European Market and Jim Rader, who handled Advertising for ROW (Rest of the World). The ROW markets, also known as AMESA, included Africa, the Middle-East and South America. Over time the ROW markets grew to include Asia Pacific. Both Tom and Jim were former AMC employees. The position I was interviewing for as the Merchandising Manager was going to be responsible for Europe and the ROW markets. The job involved overseeing all shows and exhibits, special events, training, tie-ins/cross promotions, point-of-sale materials and the development/production of promotional and collateral materials. I also met with Fred Cody, the Marketing Manager that was the decision maker and the person the position reported to. During most of the interview, he seemed preoccupied and appeared to be very busy. His desk was completely covered with paper and booklets neatly stacked in piles. While he was cordial and asked very pointed questions, you could not help but get the feeling that there was more to him than meets the eye. I left the meeting with him feeling unsure as to whether I would be offered the position. Some of the other people I met with were more for show. I met Jon Holcomb, who was the General Sales Manager for ROW, Ang Dermidoff, the Distribution Manager and Dennis Kelley the Parts and Service Director. I also met Larry Whitefield, who was previously one of Lee Iacocca's bodyguards. Larry had recently been promoted to a Coordinator position that reported to the Merchandising Manager. The only other person I met with was Julie Martinek a recent graduate from

Thunderbird that was a Coordinator for Fred Cody and the advertising guys.

Contrary to the impression I got during my interview with Fred Cody, I was offered the position and joined Chrysler International on May 15, 1989. Chrysler International was located in office space at the Sterling Heights Assembly Plant (SHAP) instead of at world headquarters in Highland Park. The first week at work I discovered what a huge task it was going to be to re-launch Chrysler with such a small team. I was also beginning to get a glimpse into an even bigger problem, and that was Fred Cody's temperament. He could go from being intensely focused to a full out blow-up in a matter of minutes without any warning or apparent provocation. At times he was absolutely brilliant and other times completely irrational. He was definitely a Dr. Jekyll and Mr. Hyde. I later found out that he came from a very wealthy but dysfunctional family. His mother died when he was fairly young, and he was raised along with his three sisters by his father and stepmother. His father and uncle were bigwigs in the publishing business and there was a high school in Detroit named after his grandfather. His uncle Bernd Cody was a close friend of Lee Iacocca, which Fred repeatedly used to his advantage. I heard from several reliable sources that Fred had been a hard drinking and mean-spirited drunk who stopped drinking after his wife threatened to leave him. He didn't stop by taking the traditional approach of going through Alcoholics Anonymous' 12-Step program. Instead, he just quit drinking. Fred was what some people call a "dry drunk," which is someone who abstains from drinking using willpower alone. He never worked on the problems or issues that caused him to drink, made major lifestyle changes or developed a support group or system. He just quit. The problem with doing it that way is that you are still left with the same explosive and erratic behavior common for most alcoholics even though you stopped drinking.

163

The task of re-launching Chrysler would have been impossible without the support of Bozell Worldwide; Campbell, Mithun and Esty (CME) and Ross Roy. Bozell was the lead agency responsible primarily for Chrysler Advertising and the development of all product brochures and catalogues. Jeep Advertising was handled by CME. Ross Roy, which was more of a marketing firm oversaw the production of data books, the training program and point-of-sale materials for dealer showrooms. Leo Kelmenson was the Chairman of Bozell and very close friends with Lee Iacocca. Tom Benghauser was the Managing Director from Bozell, overseeing management of our account. He had a young lady named Laurel Zimmerman working for him, as well as Brian Kaye, who was our Account Executive. Mike Vogel headed up CME and Tom Bernardin was the Vice President assigned to us. Reporting to Tom and calling on our group were Brian Green and Jerry Acciaioli. Dick Ward was the President of Ross Roy and Rex Smith was the Vice President in charge of the Chrysler International account. Rex's Account Management team included Julia Francke, Terry Spilos and Dan Bennett.

Throughout the years, we saw agency personnel come and go. Tom Benghauser, who was rumored to have had a nervous breakdown, was replaced by Calvin Mew. Calvin was a Vice President of Bozell - hand picked for the job by Leo Kelmenson. Leo thought Calvin, who was a graduate of Yale, would be able to deal with Fred intellectually and possibly minimize some of the emotional stress. Although Calvin came as close as anyone to becoming a confidant of Fred's, it didn't help to reduce the emotional outbreaks. When Calvin moved on in 1994, he was replaced by Jim Moore. Jim had tons of agency experience and was easy to work with, but it didn't matter when it came to Fred. Jim later became the President of Leo Burnett Detroit responsible for the General Motors account. Things with Ross Roy were relatively stable with no changes in our Account Management team other than the departure of Dan Bennett. On the Jeep side, Tom Bernardin went on to bigger and better things. He is currently the CEO of Leo Burnett Worldwide. He was replaced by Harry Grusche, a mild mannered executive, who like everyone else, found it extremely difficult to deal with Fred.

Typical of how most foreign automotive manufactures initiate operations in other countries/markets, we worked through distributors instead of dealers. We franchised the distributors who in turn selected and franchised the dealers. We had an office, Chrysler Automotive Services (CAS) in Dreieich just outside of Frankfurt, Germany that called on the distributors. At first it was headed up by Klaus Hadulla and later by Gene Heidemann. When I arrived, we had distributor operations in the following European countries: Germany, Belgium, Holland, Austria, Switzerland, Sweden and Denmark. We later expanded to include France, Spain, Italy, Greece, Finland, Norway, Iceland and much later the United Kingdom. In the ROW markets, we were just beginning to secure distributors in South America. The process of securing ROW distributors and one for the U.K. was much slower, primarily because we did not have right-hand drive (RHD) products, which several of these markets required.

One of the earlier and larger distributors was Evert Louwman (a Dutchman) who owned the distributor operations in Germany, Belgium and Holland. Evert continued the tradition of importing American cars started by his father P. W. Louwman in 1934. Through his company, Louwman and Parqui Car Importships, his father imported the first Dodge vehicle into Holland. In addition to Evert's many holdings, he owns the Louwman Museum in Raamsdonksveer. It is one of the world's largest private car collections and the oldest personal collection open to the public in Europe. I had the honor of facilitating a contribution to the Museum. In 1991 Evert Louwman opened a Parts Depot in Born, Netherlands. I was asked by Fred to find a suitable gift that Lee Iacocca could give Evert during the inauguration ceremony. The challenge was finding a suitable gift for someone who had everything. I remembered him telling the story about how, when he was a little boy, he would come to Detroit with his father to purchase vehicles. They would go to the old Chalmers Plant on Jefferson Avenue in Detroit to conduct business. He talked about driving underneath the old clock that sat on the bridge-way that connected the office and display building to the rest of the manufacturing complex. At the time I was looking for a gift, they were in the process of demolishing the building, and I got the bright idea to go down and see if there might be some memento that I could find. When I arrived, they had just completed tearing down the bridge-way, and I asked where the old clock was. I was directed to go see the construction foreman, who pointed to it sitting in a pile of rubbish waiting to be discarded. Remarkably, it was still intact and appeared to be in good condition. I asked if I could take it and was told no, unless I got permission from someone high up in Chrysler. I immediately went back to Fred with the idea of having the clock restored and sent to Evert as a gift. He loved the idea and placed a call to Iacocca's office and before the day was over the clock was put aside for me. I hired a local iron sculptor in Detroit named Richard Bennett to completely refinish, mount and engrave the clock with an inscription. When the clock was presented to Everet Louwman it literally brought tears to his eyes. He was told the story by Fred of how and why I got the clock, and from that day forward he always called me "my friend the clock man."

Working in concert with CAS, it was our job to work with the distributors to launch the various Chrysler and Jeep branded products. There was no need to assist them with launch related operations since most of them already had operations in place handling other brands. In Europe, we did not use the Dodge or Plymouth brand name, although the product lines included several derivatives from these brands. In 1989 the product lineup included the Jeep Products (Cherokee and Wrangler); the Chrysler Voyager (minivan); the Chrysler LeBaron and the Dodge Spirit (re-

166

badged as a Chrysler Saratoga in Europe). In the case of the Chrysler Voyager, it was available in both a gas and diesel engine version. Back then in Europe, diesels accounted for around 50-60 percent of sales in many markets. The other important factor to note is that the brand in Europe was considered very upscale, and enjoyed the benefit of the American mystique. Jeep was legendary and iconic and Chrysler epitomized American style and quality engineering.

Working for Fred Cody was like walking through a land mine. One moment he was focused and calm and the next moment he would blow up yelling, screaming and hyperventilating. On Monday mornings, we had our weekly staff meeting. The meeting included me, Jim Rader, Tom Draur and Julie Martinek, as well as representatives from Bozell, CME and Ross Roy. We would start out with Fred reviewing the priorities and assignments for each of us. Then each one of us would provide a status update on the projects we were working on. Invariably, during one of our reviews Fred would get antsy and interrupt you. He would insist that you hurry up, because according to him, you were wasting time. It didn't matter whether it was one of us or Tom Benghauser, Tom Bernardin, or Rex Smith. The criticism from Fred was never constructive; it was always demeaning and felt personal. It was like being humiliated by your parents in front of your friends. His anger was so intense that one day he was upset and yelling at someone on the phone; he got up and slammed his office door, causing the glass wall his door was attached to, to completely shatter.

His bad behavior was not limited to his direct reports and the agencies. It even included the distributors. One year during our annual fall distributor meetings in November to review their marketing plans for the upcoming year, the distributor in Austria did a lousy job of presenting their plan. In an act of frustration, halfway through their presentation Fred got up, took his copy of the presentation and tore it into little pieces. He went on to tell them it was the worst presentation he had ever seen, and then walked out of the room. Devastated by his reaction, they hired a new Marketing Manager whose first name was Ingo. He was well educated, polished, and his English was impeccable. The following year he presented their marketing plan, and it was superb. At the end of the presentation he looked at Fred and thanked him for his patience, before handing him a nicely wrapped business gift as a token of their appreciation. Fred accepted the gift and was about to put it in his briefcase when Ingo asked him to open the gift now. Inside of a box was the front cover of the presentation he tore in pieces, framed. Ingo said to him that this was a reminder of how far they had come in a year. We all laughed and looked at Fred, who was also smiling.

The obvious question that anyone would have is how Fred could get away with this kind of behavior in Corporate America. He got away with it because he was the only one in Senior Management that was not afraid or intimidated by Iacocca. Whenever we needed Iacocca's approval of anything marketing related Fred made the presentation and for the most part, was able to secure his approval. Everyone thought it was because of the relationship that Iacocca had with his uncle, Bernd Cody. There were countless times that I thought Fred's behavior was going to get him fired. Initially, our group reported to Mike Hammes, the VP of International Operations. Big Mike, whose office was in Highland Park on Executive Row, didn't like Fred, but he respected his enormous capacity and ability to get things done. For him, it was more advantageous to ignore Fred than to do something about him. When we got a new Vice President of International, Joe Cappy, who was the prior President of AMC, I was sure things were going to be different. In fact, he brought in Pat Smorra as the new General Manager of International. He was previously the Regional Manager of the California zone. Pat's office was at SHAP, and he had a reputation for being tough. He was an ex-marine that everybody secretly called "The Blade." Pat soon realized that International was a great place to be with tons of perks. He loved the travel and playing on a much bigger stage with distributors, who had all sorts of toys at their disposal. Fred represented a huge conundrum for Pat. He made his job easy, because he could handle the big boss (Iacocca), and he was a workaholic. His solution to the problem was to give Ralph Sarrotti, the Director brought in to oversee Product Development (who was a friend of Joe Cappy's), responsibility for Marketing, including controlling Fred. Ralph was his new scape-goat. Under Pat, sales grew from 61,905 units in 1991 to 105,849 in 1993.

Despite the challenges with Fred, we launched product after product in market after market, and it was done flawlessly. Our sales continued to grow monthly by double digits. We were on a roll and so was the corporation. My department (Merchandising) was repeatedly hitting its stride in all areas. We had a new team member, Mike Zdonek, who replaced Larry Whitefield. Mike was from the Los Angeles Region and had worked for Pat Smorra. Mike was new to Shows and Exhibits and Special Events, but he was committed and a fast learner. My hard work and achievements were being noticed and appreciated; especially given the nature of the work environment with Fred. My relationship with the distributors and the agencies was great. I got along extremely well with both Ralph Sarrotti and Pat Smorra. Oftentimes they would call me in and ask me how things are going when they heard through one of their sources that Fred had gone off. They kept reassuring me that they were going to do something about Fred and to hang in there. One time I went to them and told them they were going to have to do something about him soon. Mike Zdonek, who most would describe as even-tempered, came to me one day after being ripped by Fred and asked me where he could get a gun. I knew he was not serious, but I also knew that he had reached a point of frustration, and something needed to be done. Pat called Fred into his office, gave him a tongue-lashing and restricted his travel. For the next months, they completely bypassed Fred. Instead of going to him, Ralph and Pat went to his direct reports.

International Operations provided me with a global and unique perspective of the world and the automotive industry. I coordinated, and was party to, several potentially industry-changing events. I helped arrange one of the first serious meetings between Lee Iacocca and Kirk Kerkorian at the 1992 Winter Olympics in Albertville, France. I had to make arrangements at the last minute to get a slip for Kerkorian's yacht. In 1993, long before any talks with Daimler about a merger, I worked on a dinner hosted by Norbert Wagner, the head of Sonauto, our new distributor in France. Norbert was a cousin of Ferdinand Piech, the grandson of Ferdinand Porsche and married to a member of the Getrag transmission family. He had a huge dinner party at his estate, and the invited guests included Ferdinand Piech from Porsche; Carl Hahn the Chairman of Volkswagen; a member of the Agnelli family, the owners of Fiat and Heinz Prechter from American Sunroof. It was clear that this was more than a social event. Chrysler was shopping for a partner, and they were interested.

In the midst of everything going on at International, Rita and I got married in 1991. We decided to forgo the big wedding and instead went for a civil ceremony. Our marriage was a long time coming and some would say without a lot of pomp and circumstance. At this stage in our lives, we didn't require it because the one thing we knew for sure was that our love was meant to be. To celebrate our marriage, we took a cruise with one of Rita's closest friends, Dorothy Purifoy and her husband, Bill. We were living in a two-bedroom apartment in a building called Garden Court located at 2900 East Jefferson Avenue. The building was a couple of blocks from the river and about three minutes east of downtown Detroit. The building was listed on the National Register of Historic Places. It had huge spacious luxury apartments that in its heyday were home to the Ford family and

170

many other prominent Detroit families. The building was featured in the television show Martin. Eventually, we moved from our two-bedroom apartment to a 2,500 square foot unit on the fifth floor. It was a three-bedroom unit with a large foyer, a living room with wood-burning fireplace and a view of the river, a den/study and formal dining room and a kitchen with a large butler's pantry. There was wainscoting and hardwood floors throughout. It was our perfect love nest in the middle of the city.

#

There were many days that I left work questioning why I put up with all the crap from Fred. I knew that in spite of the difficulty working with him that this was a rare and unique opportunity to be a part of a team transforming and reshaping the face of a company globally that very few kids from the inner city ever get to experience. For me, it was about persevering and winning the prize in the end.

I Corinthian 9:24-27 says, "Do you not know that in a race all the runners run, but only one receives the prize? So run that you may obtain it. Every athlete exercises self-control in all things. They do it to receive a perishable wreath, but we do it to receive an imperishable one. So I do not run aimlessly; I do not box as one beating the air. But I discipline my body and keep it under control, lest after preaching to others, I myself should be disqualified."

Sterling Heights Assembly Plant (SHAP)

171

Fred K. Cody Jr.

Calvin Mew

Dinner with European colleagues

Lee Iacocca

173

Louwman Museum

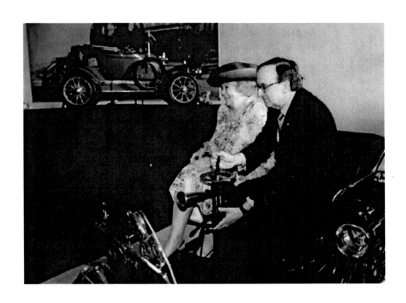

Evert Louwman at the museum with the queen

NORWEGIAN CRUISE LINE   M/S SEAWARD

Alvin and Rita – honeymoon cruise

Storming the Bastille and
Taking Back the Distribution Rights

Working overseas or being an expatriate was a benefit and privilege reserved for the best and brightest with the highest potential. The benefits at the time included an overseas allowance, which was an incentive paid to you when you were repatriated back to the U.S. In underdeveloped countries your assistance could include a hardship allowance on top of your overseas allowance. The size of the allowance, which could be a rather large amount, depended on how many months you worked overseas. I've known individuals that were on multiple assignments totaling upwards of 13 years. You also received a cost of living allowance paid to you monthly with your paycheck, which considered the difference between the average cost of goods and services in your home city in the U.S. versus the city/country where you were assigned. There was also a rent subsidy to help offset the higher cost of rent for a housing unit in that country. For example, the rent on your in-country unit could be the equivalent of $4,500 U.S. dollars, and you would only have to pay $1,500, even though the rent on the unit where you lived in the U.S. was $2,000 or $2,500. Depending on what country you were being sent to and whether you had kids or not, the benefits could include private school for your school age kids and a car with driver and security.

It gave you a glimpse into a whole different world and provided you with a perspective that typically only industry captains and leaders get to experience. If you were selected for an overseas assignment it meant that you were highly regarded and viewed as a future leader. In 1991, Julie Martinek from our group was sent to work in the newly opened office in Paris. Christian Dubus, the Managing Director of the office, was good with sales, but not with marketing or maintaining the processes and procedures

176

required by the home office back in the U.S. Julie's job was to handle the marketing and oversee the implementation of the processes and procedures. The other person from International Operations to receive an overseas assignment was Mike Zdonek, who worked for me. Mike was sent to Italy in 1992 to open up a satellite office in Milan in conjunction with the signing on of two new distributors in Italy and Greece. The satellite office in Milan reported to Christian Dubus, whose job title had been changed to Managing Director for Southern Europe responsible for France, Spain, Italy and Greece.

In May 1993, Pat Smorra called me into to his office and said, "Al, I know you have been working hard and looking for a promotion. Unfortunately, right now I can't give you a promotion because of some things that are going on in the company, but there is another way I can help you." He went on to explain that Chrysler was seriously considering buying back the distribution rights from the distributors in Europe, and that they were probably going to start with the distributor in France, Sonauto. He wanted me to go to France and work out of the office in Paris reporting to Christian Dubus. My official job title would be "Commerciale Directeur" for France and Spain responsible for sales and marketing. My unofficial responsibility was to take control of the relationship with Sonauto and get to know the dealers. Our relationship with Sonauto was out of control; they were dictating to us instead of vice-versa. It was a bad case of the tail wagging the dog. Their Marketing Director, Franck Metzger, was very opinionated. He was constantly clashing with Fred Cody and the agencies over everything from the creative to the media buy, as well as how we allocated dollars to support their market. Pat wanted to put a stop to that, and he wanted to know more about the strength of their dealer network, which he believed was the essence of what you purchase when buy back distribution rights.

177

He said he would make sure I got a nice raise, plus I would receive all the benefits associated with being an expatriate, but it would not include a grade level increase which is what I wanted. I was already a grade-band 94, which was the beginning grade for IC (incentive compensation/bonus payments) and desperately working to become a 95 (the same level as Fred Cody). I discussed the matter with Rita and we both agreed that although it was not everything I wanted, it was too good of an offer to pass up. The only real downside was that it would make it impossible for me to continue seeing my daughter Alyssa every other weekend, which was part of my visitation rights in the custody agreement. However, we were looking forward to having her come visit us in Paris. The company would pay for three trips per year for kids left behind. The problem was that she was only nine years old, and I anticipated her mother having a problem with her traveling alone, being so young.

Upon saying yes to Pat the whirlwind began. I had to finish up all the projects I was working on, meet with HR and start the process of completing all the paperwork required to live and work in France. There were of course, all the customary bon voyage parties that I had to attend put on by our friends and my colleagues. The plan was for me to start work in Paris Monday, October 18. My last day in the office was scheduled for Thursday July 29 and the following week we were scheduled to fly to Paris for our "look-see trip" to find housing. After that we took the next two weeks getting everything ready for the movers. August 23 we had to begin our 6-week language immersion program in Cincinnati, Ohio, before going to Chicago for two days of Cross-Cultural training and visiting the French Consulate to finalize our documentation. Every moment of our life was scheduled out.

Our look-see trip to Paris was interesting in that it was Rita's first trip abroad. Even though she kept saying she was excited about living in Paris, I was a little worried about how she was going to make the

178

adjustment. We flew out Friday evening July 30th and arrived the following morning. We wanted to arrive during the weekend so that we would be fully acclimated by Monday, when were to meet the representatives from Corporate Relocation, who would be taking us around. When we arrived there was a huge strike, which included the sanitation workers at the airport. The airport was an absolute mess with the garbage cans full and garbage strewn everywhere. You talk about first impressions; based on this, Rita's first impression of Paris was not good. After picking up our baggage and clearing customs, we got a cab to the Le Méridien Etoile Hotel. In an effort to try to quickly change her perspective of Paris, that evening, I took her on a dinner cruise down the Seine River on the Bateaux Mouche. It did help to change her perspective; I could tell all of this was a little overwhelming and producing a lot of anxiety for both of us. On Sunday, we just relaxed and walked up to the Champs Elysees and Saint-Honore and Avenue Montaigne where most of the high-end shops in Paris are located.

On Monday morning, we met with Martinez Jones the representative from Corporate Relocation assigned to help us find housing and assist with our relocation. Marty was French and married to an Englishman. The first day we spent touring potential areas, and quickly decided that we didn't want to live in Neuilly-sur-Seine (Neuilly) where all the other American expats lived, and our office was located. After some discussion, we agreed that moving into Neuilly would make getting acclimated to the French culture too difficult. Most Americans who moved into Neuilly did so because it was the home of many large American corporations and close to the American School where most of their children attended. It was also known for catering to Americans. Since this was not a consideration for us, plus the fact that we wanted to experience as much of the French lifestyle as possible, we decided to remove Neuilly from our list of potential areas. The two areas we decided we were most interested in were the 8th and 17th Arrondissements. Paris is divided into 20 arrondissements or municipal administrative districts. The 8th Arrondissement was called Elysee and is situated on the right bank of the River Seine centered on the Opéra. The 8th together with the 2nd and 9th Arrondissements is one of Paris' main business districts. It is also the location of many places of interest such as the Champs-Élysées, the Arc de Triomphe and the Place de la Concorde, as well as the Élysée Palace, the official residence of the President of France. The 17th Arrondissement, which is also on the right bank, is made up of three areas. In the extreme southeastern part is a working-class area around Place de Clichy, which is an extension of the Pigalle red-light district. Then there is Montmartre in the southwestern part that is home to Sacre-Coeur Basilica, one of Paris's major tourist attractions. The third area, known as an upper-class area, included streets like Avenue des Ternes, Avenue de Wagram and Avenue de la Grande-Armée.

After looking at apartments in both arrondissements; we decided on one located in the 17th at 17 Rue Alphonse de Neuville between Wagram and Boulevard Pereire. It was a large building with a cobblestone court yard. The apartment we selected was off the courtyard located on the first floor which we would consider being the second floor. It was a three-bedroom 2,500 square foot apartment with beautiful marble fireplaces in each bedroom and in the living room and dining room. It had large plank parquet floors throughout and two brand new bathrooms. Each room had windows at least seven feet tall. The living and dining rooms had cove ceilings with intricate moldings and carvings on the walls and ceilings. What I found most interesting was that the apartments did not come with light fixtures or a finished kitchen. As the tenant you were required to purchase and install your own light fixtures, which you took with you when you vacated the apartment. Typically, all you would find in any apartment was an electrical wire with a light bulb at the end of it or capped off wires where

180

you would normally have wall sconces. The kitchen would typically just have a free standing sink and gas or electrical lines. Everything else that went into a kitchen you were responsible for providing: from the kitchen cabinets, sink and countertops to the appliances. In looking for an apartment it was important that you not only see it in the daytime but also at night, because oftentimes it could be totally different. There was one apartment that we were strongly considering in the 8th Arrondissement until we visited it at night and realized the street where it was located was frequented by prostitutes.

With the finding of an apartment and the completion of the look-see trip, all that was left was to return to the U.S. and start getting ready for the move. One thing we needed to do was to secure appliances and other electronics. We had learned through Mike Zdonek, that there was a company in Chicago that sold European spec'd appliances and electronic equipment for a lot less than what you could buy them for in-country. Even though Chrysler was paying for them, there was no reason not to try to save the company some money. He and his wife Debbie purchased their items from this company and saved anywhere from 25-35 percent. We compiled a list of all the things we needed, and via phone and fax, were able to finalize the selection and arrangements to have them shipped to the same location stateside where our household goods were going. The plan was to have them incorporated with the rest of the shipment for us going to Paris.

As tedious and tiresome as it was, we got everything organized and ready for the packers who arrived on Tuesday, August 17. The actual move occurred two days later on Thursday and Friday. We left Detroit Saturday morning and flew to Cincinnati, where we checked into a hotel until we were able to find a short-term rental. On Monday morning, we reported to inlingua to begin our six weeks of language immersion. I knew going in it was going to be tough, especially for Rita. She was a nurse with a strong science background who did not take a language in high school or college. I, on the other hand, had studied French in both. We were each assigned a different teacher and told from this point forward everything was going to be in French, including the instructions. At lunchtime, we looked forward to eating together and being able to speak to each other in English. To our surprise, we discovered that our instructors accompanied us to lunch and forced us to communicate with each other in French during lunch. We also learned that we would be in class six days a week. The Saturday class was only for a half-day. While it was tough for me, it was excruciatingly difficult for Rita. She could understand what was being said to her, but was having a difficult time with pronunciation, and especially with the rolling "r's" known to linguists as the alveolar trill. At the end of everyday she would have an excruciating headache from trying to concentrate on correctly pronouncing the language. I felt sorry for her, but she held in there to the bitter end.

Friday, August 20 was our last day at Inlingua. We took a flight to Chicago that night and checked into the Swiss Grand Hotel on Wacker Drive. Friends of ours, Dorothy and Bill Purifoy, had planned a bon voyage party for us on Saturday at a club on the South Side and invited most of our friends from Chicago. I had made a special request that they try to locate and invite my old high school French teacher, Mr. William Hunter. I wanted to make sure I got a chance to apologize to him for not paying more attention when I was in his class. I was required to take a language in high school, and I selected French, never thinking I would ever need to be able to speak it fluently. Mr. Hunter, who had retired some years earlier, showed up at the party, and I was able to publicly apologize to him. He got a big kick out of it. The following Monday we started our Cross-Cultural Training and Orientation Program. The first day was okay as they talked about French culture in general. However, during the second and final day, when the discussion shifted to what to expect and began to focus more on

182

negative things, I could tell Rita was becoming a little irritated. They were saying things like the French can be very rude and standoffish, and that we should not expect to get to know our neighbors or have many French friends. My wife, who is a people-person, was offended; by the way they depicted the French. What troubled her most was the generalization that we should not look forward to making friends. She looked at me and said, "I think this is a waste of Chrysler's money. Who are they to say what will or will not happen for us? I have had enough; I am going shopping for the rest of the afternoon and will see you back at the hotel." We left Chicago Wednesday night and arrived in Paris Thursday morning October 7 to begin our new life.

We checked into the Le Méridien Etoile Hotel, the same one we stayed in during our look-see trip. Claude Germain, one of my colleagues from the office in Paris, left a car at the hotel for us. We were pretty tired from all the activities leading up to this point, so we spent Thursday and Friday lounging around the hotel. On Friday, we got word that the sea container with all of our belongings was going to be delivered to our new apartment on Monday. We remained in the hotel for the rest of the weekend, and early Monday morning checked out of the hotel and went to the new apartment to meet the movers. Rita had started to relax and didn't want to leave the hotel. She kept saying – "why can't we just go to the apartment and start unpacking and then come back to the hotel when everything was unpacked and put away." I told her sorry, but Chrysler would never agree to it, and that it was time for us to take the next step in moving forward. We spent the rest of the week getting unpacked and running back and forth to stores to pick up various things we needed to get settled in.

The first week at my new office, which was located at 41 Rue Ybry in Neuilly, was less traumatic than the move itself, primarily because I had worked with the staff before coming. My new boss, Christian Dubus, the

183

Managing Director of the office, was French Canadian. He was tall, about 6'1" or 6'2," with silver hair and could be very charming and disarming. He was a Canadian version of Maurice Chevalier, with an eye for the ladies. Claude Germain, the Distribution Manager who was originally from California, was married to a French national he met while working as a flight attendant at British Airways. Claude was a high-energy "let's get it done" type of guy who I became close friends with. We had a strong mutual respect for each other developed from our years working together on the Paris Motor Show.

The other Manager in the office was Pierre LeCount, who was in charge of parts and service. Prior to joining Chrysler, I think he worked for GM. He was a nice guy who seemed committed to doing a good job. The administrative staff consisted of Mariam, Paschale and Anne Noury. Mariam, who I think was from the Ivory Coast, was quiet and kept to herself. Paschale was just the opposite; she was very outgoing and talkative. She was responsible for keeping the books and paying the bills. Anne Noury was Mr. Dubus' secretary and considered herself to be the Office Manager. Anne, who was young, extremely attractive and very flirtatious, had a reputation for being a "B." It wasn't long after I arrived that I had my first of many run-ins with her. I gave her a few things to type, and it came back horrible. It was as if she didn't even try to get it right. When I kept giving it back to her and complaining she was quick to tell me that she was not my secretary and only doing this as a favor. When I brought the matter up with Christian, he said, "You know how Anne is, and maybe you might want to consider the company purchasing you a laptop" which were just becoming popular. At first I didn't give the idea much thought, but later on when it became obvious that the situation was not going to improve, I acquiesced and got a laptop. I later suspected that Anne was more than just Christian's secretary; perhaps she was his laptop, and I needed my own.

It did not take me long to build a good working relationship with Sonauto, our distributor in France, and establish who was in charge. I would have weekly meetings with them to review their sales and marketing efforts. Franck Metzger, the Marketing Director, who was born the exact same day that I was, respected and appreciated my sales and marketing knowledge and listened to what I had to say. Through me the relationship between Sonauto and the agency improved and so did the relationship with Fred Cody. I anticipated and worked through many of the potential contentious issues and kept things on track. I was even able to work through some of the internal strife between Franck Metzger and their new Sales Manager, Reginald Lyon-Lynch. Overall, I got more things done with them, and as a result saw significant increases in sales.

On the personal side, our apartment was coming together nicely after a few challenges communicating with workers about things we needed to get done. Rita was building relationships with the shop owners in the community, and it was becoming easier for her to get what she wanted from the boulangerie (bakery), fleuriste (florist), nettoyeurs à sec (dry cleaners) and bucherie (butcher). The people from Corporate Relocation initially went with her to introduce her to the various shop owners, and she took it from there. The branch of the Credit Lyonnais bank that we did business with was in Neuilly, and they were very helpful to Rita with any transactions we needed to get done. Rita had also developed a good relationship with the building concierge, who spoke very little English, but was very helpful. For someone who was challenged speaking the language, she was doing remarkably well getting things done. She had even begun to meet wives of other expats that she was able to become friends with. During the last couple of weeks in Cincinnati at Inlingua, we met Jerry and Sue Fowler, who were also being sent to Paris. Jerry worked for General Motors as an engineer and his wife Sue was an attorney. They had a young daughter named Allie. Rita ran into Sue at one of the meetings she attended put on by an organization called "Bloom Where You're Planted." Rita and Sue became good friends and spent a lot of time together. Through that same organization, she met a Black couple, Mark and Michele Latney from Indianapolis. Mark worked for a company called Thompson Electronics in procurement and supply. Like Rita and me, it was just the two of them.

One day when I was back in the states for meetings, I got a call from Rita to tell me that she had met a new friend for me. When she was in the dry cleaners picking up my shirts, which by the way, they charged the equivalent of five dollars to launder, she over heard a Black man complaining to the owner about the way his shirts were being laundered. She could not figure out exactly what he was saying because he was speaking French with an unusual accent. However, she could tell he was not happy with the small wrinkles (I call them cat faces) all over his shirts. On several occasions, I had complained to Rita that we were paying too much per shirt to have them come back with "cat faces." She waited outside the cleaners for the man to come out and asked him – "are you an American?" - and he said "yes." He introduced himself and told her he was Warren Wiltz. She told him that her husband was complaining about the same thing. They chatted a little more, and she learned that he and his wife Valencia lived on Boulevard Pereire diagonally across from where we lived. She invited him to come by so that she could meet his wife. They were from New Orleans, and he worked for UPS. When I returned to Paris from the states, they invited us over so I could meet them. Warren was about four years younger than me. His wife Valencia, who was very attractive, was younger than him. She was tall with long pretty jet-black hair and appeared to be what some might call high maintenance. She turned out to be much more, and we have remained friends ever since that day and believe it or not, are currently neighbors in Atlanta. They in turn introduced us to another expat couple, Dan and Minion Weaver, who also lived in the

186

17th Arrondissement not far from us. They had a small son, Mikey. Dan was a Ph.D. and worked in research for a company whose name escapes me, for the moment. His wife Minion ended up attending Cordon Bleu which is a world renowned cooking school.

Living in Paris meant relearning how to do many things, including driving. Driving in Paris is tantamount to being in a roller derby, especially when you enter the roundabouts or traffic circles. In France the car to the right of you always has the right of way, which is counterintuitive. In the U.S., roundabouts require entering drivers to yield to the traffic already in the roundabout, regardless of lane position, while traffic circles typically allow traffic to enter alongside traffic circulating in an inner lane without consequence. Initially, Rita was hesitant about driving because of the crazy way the Parisians drove; especially in the roundabouts or traffic circles. I had suggested on several occasions that she might want to consider taking driving lessons. I think she was contemplating taking lessons but decided at the last moment that she didn't need them. One Sunday we were at the outdoor market in Neuilly. As I was entering our Grand Cherokee on the driver's side, Rita said – "wait I want to drive." I was surprised but moved to the passenger side and proceeded to ask, "Are you sure you don't want to take lessons first." Her response was, "Did you need to take lessons before you started driving?" The answer to her question was no. From that day forward she drove wherever she needed to go when the car was available, unless it made more sense to take the Metro (rapid transit system).

After having been in the office in Neuilly for only a few months, it was decided by the home office that we should look for larger and nicer office accommodations. Our lease on the location in Neuilly was expiring, and it did not make sense to renew it. The office space we had was too small to handle the larger staff anticipated when we bought back the distribution rights, plus it was not the right image for an upscale brand. The space and building we were in, felt more like a government office than an office location for a major corporation the size of Chrysler. We concentrated our search for a new office location in the more fashionable areas like the 8th and 17th Arrondissements, which just so happened to be the same areas where Christian and I lived. After visiting multiple locations we decided on a recently renovated building at 42 Avenue de la Grande-Armée in the 17th. It was within five minutes of where Christian lived and ten minutes from where I lived. It was down the street from the headquarters of PSA Peugeot Citroën and just up the street from the Arc de Triomphe and the Champs-Élysées. We had more than ample space to accommodate the present staff as well as the larger anticipated staff. We had the entire fifth floor of the building. When you came off the elevator, the main office was to the left, and to the right was additional office space to accommodate the planned expansion. Christian had a spacious open office on one end of a large glassed in conference room, and I had a smaller but nice office on the other end. Our offices and the conference room faced Avenue de la Grande-Armée with each having a balcony that provided a clear view of the Arc de Triomphe.

While I was getting settled into life in Paris, there were a lot of changes taking place back at the home office. Pat Smorra had left the company and purchased a dealership in Napa Valley shortly after I got to Paris. He allegedly had a run-in with Bob Lutz about the timing of buying back the distribution rights. Pat, who was not 100 percent convinced that we would do a better job if we took control, wanted to wait and Bob Lutz wanted to accelerate the process. Lutz got his way and Pat paid the price for disagreeing with the boss. Pat was replaced by Tim Adams, who prior to coming to International, spent most of his time working on the Alfa Romeo and Lamborghini projects. Unlike Pat Smorra, he was not a real sales or dealer guy with strong practical experience. He was more of a business development type that was definitely more theoretical and philosophical about everything. It took him forever to make a decision; everything needed to have a consensus reached and triangulated. He was appointed by Lutz to make the buyback of distribution rights happen faster with the operative word being faster, which was contrary to his nature. Unfortunately, it wasn't long before Bob Lutz realized that Tim was not the one to make it happen faster, and he was replaced by Darryl Davis. Darryl was a cigar chomping Coca Cola drinking good-ole-boy. He worked his way up the corporate ladder starting out as Dealership Mechanic into the Corporate Parts and Service Department with the manufacturer and from there went into Corporate Sales. He was the great American success story and had all the toys to prove it. He was in a semi-retirement mode living in a large home in Florida before he got the assignment to head up International. The home in Florida was especially built to house his rather large collection of antique cars he had amassed. When he got the assignment he refused to move back to Michigan and instead got a small apartment and flew into the office in Michigan every week when he was not out traveling.

As the home office was undergoing its fair share of challenges, I was dealing with a few of my own. Our ability to be able to grow our sales was constrained to a great extent by the dealers' ability to get the capital; which they needed to expand their facilities. A lot of our planned sales growth was going to come from expanding the product offering, which meant the dealers needed more showroom space and bigger parts and service areas. The problem was that in 1995, automotive sales in Europe were beginning to slow down, and the banks were less inclined to provide funding for expansion. The conundrum that I was faced with was that although sales in general were down for most dealers, they were up for Chrysler dealers. Somehow, I needed to be able to get to the bankers to tell our story, which was not one of decline, but in fact, just the opposite. I mentioned the dilemma, I was having to a colleague I had been working with from the U.S. Department of Commerce in Paris. On several occasions, he had said to me that if we needed help with anything that his

189

office and the U.S. Ambassador to France, Pamela Harriman were available to assist in whatever way possible. He and I discussed various ways to get the word out to the French bankers that our situation was very different from the norm. The problem was that the bankers are a very independent group and would not respond to most requests to meet with them, unless it came from the right person. A simple invitation to attend a meeting to discuss the viability of Chrysler dealers coming from Chrysler Corporation or the distributor would be ignored and viewed as self-serving.

During one of our brainstorming sessions, we came up with the bright idea "what if the invitation came from the Ambassador, and it was to a reception at her residence on Embassy Row located on Rue du Faubourg Saint-Honoré?" Everybody agreed that if it came from her, it would be more like a command performance and the kind of invitation they could not turn down. Besides being the U.S. Ambassador and the former daughter-in-law of Winston Churchill, Pamela Harriman was known throughout France for her wealth and magnificent art collection. If nothing else they would come just to see the collection. They agreed to present the idea to her staff to see if she would be willing to do this to help, and she agreed. As one of the conditions for doing this, she insisted that Lee Iacocca and Bob Lutz be a part of the reception. I had not had a chance to check their calendars but knew that they would be in town for the Paris Motor Show, which was the time we were planning on having the reception. Working with Fred Cody back at home office and Gene Heidemann, the Director of European Sales, we got it added to the agenda, and I was off and rolling. Somewhere during the process of meeting with the representatives from the Department of Commerce and her staff, I realized that it was important to have the bankers see some of the new products we were coming out with that required the dealers to expand their facilities. The courtyard area in front of her residence would be a perfect place for a small display of 4 to 5 cars. When I broached the subject with the folks from Commerce and her staff they said no, but I convinced them to just ask. I told them to convey to her that it would be very important to Mr. Lutz to be able to do a private showing for the bankers, and it would make them feel special. I knew at the time that she fancied Bob Lutz, and that I stood a better chance of getting it done if I invoked his name. It worked and she said yes with the understanding that it could not be anymore than five cars. Everything was set and the plans were coming together great until it dawned on me that with the time change, that by the time the bankers arrived for the reception it was going to be too dark for them to see the details of the cars. I needed to find a way to light the cars in the courtyard. I shared my dilemma with the team, and they said "sorry I don't know what can be done about that." I said to them the only solution is to light the cars in the courtyard, and they said once again that she would never agree to that. My reply was just ask her and let her know that we will handle all of it. We had a new auto show display that was being debuted at the Paris Auto Show. As part of the team setting up the display, we had a lighting guy coming in to do the lighting that previously did lighting for Michael Jackson. I told them to tell her that the lighting would be tastefully and professionally done with the least amount of intrusion. Reluctantly, she said yes because she realized that having cars sitting in the dark, would defeat the purpose.

The night of the event everything went perfectly. Lee Iacocca, Bob Lutz and Tom Gale (head of Product Design) along with other company officers and executives were present and accounted for. The event started with opening remarks from the Ambassador, followed by a 30-minute presentation from Lee, Bob and Tom about Chrysler International's progress and success in Europe. After the presentation, there was a receiving line with the Ambassador and our top management leading into the reception area where beverages and Hors d'ouvres were served. Most of the bankers stayed to meet our management and to see her art collection and the cars in the courtyard. It turned out to be a perfect evening, with the bankers being duly impressed with what was going on at Chrysler. During the process, there was even a surprise for me. As I was going through the receiving line with my wife, and we got to the Ambassador, her assistant said to her "This is Mr. Jackson, the man from Chrysler with all the requests." She smiled and said, "I think things went well, and I hope everyone is pleased." I thanked her and told her everybody was pleased. As I was turning to introduce my wife Rita to the Ambassador, Pamela Harriman extended her hand to Rita and said, "It's good to see you again, Rita." I was totally flabbergasted because I had no idea that Rita knew the Ambassador. The million-dollar question was from where? I later found out that my wife knew her from attending several of the Bloom Where You're Planted functions, including a ladies' tea she had recently hosted at her residence. Rita is the same lady who a couple of months earlier called me while I was working in Spain, crying and threatening to return to the U.S. because she had lost her identity and was tired of being known through her husbands. In France most women are known through their husbands. Rita didn't like the idea of having to depend on me for everything, even though there was never an issue with it. She liked having her independence and having a job to earn her own money, which she was restricted from doing in France.

After we became fully acclimated, life on a personal level was great. We had good friends and plenty of money to shop, enjoy the restaurants and travel throughout Europe. We took personal trips to Frankfurt, Brussels, Amsterdam, London, Milan, Florence and Rome. I attended the French Open at Roland Garros and various major events in Paris. My wife, who became the Treasurer for the Bloom Where You're Planted group, toured on a weekly basis the various attractions in and around Paris. Sometimes it was hard to keep up with her.

The one thing we were never short on was visitors. When you live in Paris all your friends and their friends want to come visit. There was always someone visiting, or scheduled to visit from the U.S. Rita's mother, Leontine Sutton visited on a regular basis and then there was her Aunt Evelyn, as well as Shirley and Maceo Howard from Chicago. Right before we left coming back to the U.S., Bill and Pauline Adkins and their daughter Dominique came to visit. We had friends from Detroit come visit like Jackie Davis and her cousin William from Washington State. In addition, my son Richard came to visit twice, including when he was studying abroad at Loyola's Rome Center. The list goes on and on. It took a while but finally Alyssa came to visit, and we took her everywhere. In the beginning, we had problems with her mother letting her come. The original plan was to have her fly back to Paris with me; while I was in Detroit for meetings. When I called the number I had for her mother, she never returned my call and when I went to where she was last living, her boyfriend's son said they were not there anymore. I returned to Paris without her and over the next couple of months went through extreme anxiety about not being able to reach her. One night it got so bad that I could not sleep. I felt the walls closing in on me, and I could not breathe. My wife, after trying to get me to breathe into a bag to hyperventilate, called Warren in the middle of the night, to come over, and he did. For the next two hours, we walked up and down the Champs-Élysées until I finally calmed down. The next week I told my boss what was going on, and we agreed that I should take a leave of absence for a week to go back to the U.S. to find my daughter.

Speaking of daughters, in November 1994 we learned that Rita was pregnant and her due date was August 1995. Her friend Sue Fowler was also pregnant. Being pregnant did not slow down either one of them. Nor did it cause them to miss a beat. They both continued being heavily involved in their Bloom Where You're Planted activities. During her pregnancy, I tried to limit my travel to be as close to home as possible because Rita had a history of miscarriages. As one of our marketing activities every year in July we held our Jeep Jamboree in Lake Tahoe. Key

193

personnel from the distributors would participate in the event, which included four days and three nights on the trail. In all the years that I had planned the Jeep Jamboree working for Fred, I had never gone on one. The guys from Sonauto and the office were teasing me, saying that the Jeep Jamboree was too rugged for me, and that I preferred four and five star hotels. I was determined to go on this year's Jamboree as one of the corporate chaperones, especially since Christian could not go that year. I went with Rita to her doctor's appointment at the end of June to confirm that the pregnancy was going okay and there was no problem with me taking the trip. The doctor reassured me that everything was fine and Rita said go enjoy yourself. On Tuesday, July 4, 1995 I flew to Reno for the Jeep Jamboree. We spent the first couple of days at the hotel and on Friday morning got into the Jeep Wranglers and headed out. The course you take is breathtaking. It is over dusty trails, boulder-sized rocks and rushing water streams.

We returned to the hotel on Monday, July 10th and I was in the room showering trying to get rid of the dirt and dust, when I heard a loud knock at my door. It was someone from Carlson Marketing (the company that coordinated the trip) telling me a Mr. Warren Wiltz was trying to reach me to let me know that my wife was in labor. Of course, I went into a panic mode until I could reach him and found out that she had been taken to the American Hospital in Neuilly because of shortness of breath and excess swelling in her feet and legs. The Carlson Marketing staff had already started the process of trying to reschedule my flights to get me back to Paris. It was too late for me to get a flight out on Monday, so they scheduled the earliest flight leaving Tuesday morning. I flew from Reno to Las Vegas, to Minneapolis, to Chicago, to Detroit and then to Paris. Believe it or not this was the fastest way to get back to Paris. I arrived in Paris Wednesday morning at around 8:00 am and was planning on going straight to the hospital. When I called the hospital, they told me she was resting well, and that I didn't need to rush. They suggested that I go home and freshen up before coming to the hospital, which is exactly what I did. Rita was in good hands at the hospital, and Valencia was with her. Frantic Warren, on the other hand, was calling me every five minutes asking "where are you." I arrived around noon, and she was doing fine. It had already been determined that the baby could not be delivered vaginally, and that it would require a C-section. I went down with her for the epidural and then waited for her doctor to arrive. At 7:50 p.m. on July 12, 1995 our daughter Danielle Leonora Jackson was born weighing 4 lbs. 8 oz. and 17.5 inches long. Because Danielle was premature and delivered through a C-section they were going to have to be in the hospital for about 10-12 days. Later that week Alyssa arrived from the U.S. for her summer vacation. Everyday Alyssa and I would go to the hospital to have lunch with Rita and see Danielle. Eating lunch at the American Hospital was like having lunch at a five star restaurant. They had a gourmet chef and prided themselves on their excellent service. As a member of the family you could order lunch and have them deliver it with the patient's lunch. They would bring lunch and set it up on a table with white linens and flowers.

With Darryl Davis now responsible for International, the buyback of the distributor rights was fast tracked. I had already started the process of trying to get more insights on the dealer network, which from my perspective was the basis of the purchase. I set out to determine the quality of the network, so we would know how to structure the offer. It was my contention that buying back the distribution rights was like buying a dealership. You determine the value of the assets, which is a fairly simple process, and then you figure out how much blue sky you are willing to pay. The amount of blue sky paid was a multiple of the annual profits of the business. The multiplier, which is a point of negotiations, could be anywhere from 2.5 to 5 times the annual profits. In my mind, the quality of the dealers would determine whether it is 2.5 times or 5 times. I got

Sonauto to agree to my conducting an assessment of the dealers. I created the criteria for evaluating the dealers and put together a team from my office to visit all 120 dealers to conduct the assessment. When the evaluations were done I was able to report to my management how many of the dealers met the requirements from a management, capital and facility standpoint. The dealers were scored and placed in one of three categories: 1) exceeded all three requirements; 2) could meet the requirements with a little assistance from us and 3) could not meet two of the three requirements and should be terminated or not offered a franchise under the new company.

It became clear to me when the finance guys, Jerry and Keith, took up residence in our office in September 1995 that they were under extreme pressure to get the deal done at any costs. Chrysler was flush with cash and Bob Lutz wanted the purchase of Sonauto completed. They were not concerned with properly valuing the deal: all they wanted was to force Sonauto to give them a number, they would be willing to sell back the distribution rights. Sonauto was resisting giving them a number, and we were hesitant about making an offer. The plan was to wear them down until they just wanted out and came up with a number.

In the beginning of the following year, I was notified by the French Consulate that my Carte de Sejour (residency) and work permit were expiring, and that I had ninety days to get them extended or leave France. When I spoke with my management, they had no plans for extending my stay. I was told to work with HR on being repatriated back to Detroit or see if I could find an expat assignment in AMESA. In April 1996 we returned to the U.S.

#

Living and working abroad completely transformed our lives, including our way of thinking, and it broadened our perspective. We were provided with an opportunity to experience different cultures, see different places and most importantly meet and make new friends. It was a life-changing experience that even today we smile about when we think about all of our adventures.

Romans 12:2 tells us: "Do not be conformed to this world, but be transformed by the renewal of your mind, that by testing you may discern what is the will of God, what is good and acceptable and perfect."

Welcome to Paris Party

Apartment in Paris

Office in Paris

With laptop to the right

In office with Alyssa

Nina (housekeeper), Danielle and Alyssa

Fred Cody flying back to U.S. with Alyssa

Party at Ambassador's Residence

Shopping with Warren on St. Honore'

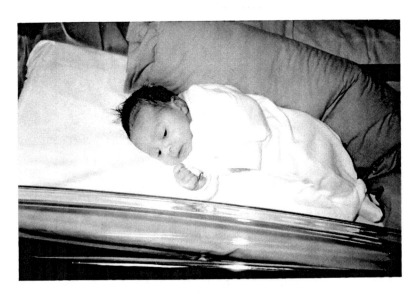

Danielle at birth

Christening

Proud parents

Warren and Valencia (Godparents) and Leontine

Party at Canne Coordinated by Fred Cody

Returning Home to a Company
Unprepared for What They Created

Chrysler, like many other Fortune 500 companies was and continues to be totally unprepared for returning expats. On one hand, they consider having international experience a key criterion for advancement into senior management, and on the other hand they don't have a plan for what to do with them when they return. There is no formal program in place to ensure that when they return the experience and knowledge gained from an overseas assignment is put to good use and continues to benefit the company in meaningful ways. As a result of this, on average, companies lose 25 percent of expats in the first year after they are repatriated. Many of those who stay end up in positions that don't properly channel or utilize their newly acquired abilities. Most companies, including Chrysler, are very reluctant to guarantee a certain job or promotion, and in many cases when you return you are placed in a temporary or holding position. This was the case when I returned from Paris. I was told that I needed to try to find a position, and in the interim I was assigned to work for Tom Wooderson, the Director of Sales Planning and Distribution for International. The good news was that Tom was sympathetic to my plight because he had been an expat and understood the challenges of returning home. The first several months were very difficult because I did not have a specific job to do, and it was tough to contain my frustration at seeing people who had never left the city, let alone the country, being promoted all around me. My job was to do whatever, he needed me to do while I looked for a position. Finding a position was difficult because other than the folks I dealt with in International, I had been out of sight and out of mind.

As much as we wanted to think of ourselves as a global company, we were just a domestic company with operations overseas. The majority of the open positions in the company were in the domestic organization, and I knew very few of the domestic guys other than the ones who occasionally traveled overseas. I reached out to all of them and was told, "it was nice to have me back", and if something comes up they would let me know. The ones who were being honest with me let me know that they had folks in their own organizations that had been waiting for a while for promotions, and that they would be given first consideration. Although that was not what I wanted to hear, I appreciated their honesty. The other problem I ran into was that many other employees, and Hiring Managers, who had never worked overseas, thought we didn't do much. They viewed us as being spoiled or arrogant based on their distorted perception that overseas assignments were glamorous, filled with all sorts of luxury benefits like servants, private schools, exotic vacations and hardship premiums. What they didn't understand was that you worked twice as hard. My normal day in the office would start around 7:30 am and oftentimes go until 9:00 or 10:00 p.m. I used to say that my second shift started around 3:00 p.m. when the U.S. employees arrived for work. I would stay late most times when I was working on projects that required input from them, which occurred frequently.

Returning to the U.S. was equally challenging for Rita. It marked the end of an exciting lifestyle she had become accustomed to, and meant having to say goodbye to friends and colleagues she met along the way. Moving back home in a lot of ways was even more dramatic than moving to Paris. Going to Paris was an exciting adventure, whereas returning was fraught with uncertainty and feelings that you didn't belong anymore because you had grown so much. In Paris, she had a great support system to help with Danielle and the luxury of not having to work. The additional income, subsidized rent, and free field car allowed us more than enough extra money for her to travel and purchase pretty much whatever she wanted. The first thing we needed to do was to find housing, and we had

207

already decided that we wanted to buy a house. Being overseas we had saved more than enough money for a decent down payment. The big question was where we wanted to live. One option was Rochester Hills, a newly developed area near our corporate offices where a lot of Chrysler executives lived. A second option was West Bloomfield, which was not as close, but had a great school system and the area was fully developed. The third option was buying a home in Palmer Woods. It was a more upscale and better maintained version of the Boston-Edison area with big old grand homes. We quickly ruled out Palmer Woods because it would more than likely require some level of renovations, which I was unwilling to entertain. We narrowed our search down to two subdivisions, one in Rochester Hills and the other in West Bloomfield. Both offered us the prospect of brand new housing, which really appealed to Rita. We ultimately decided on a spec house in West Bloomfield because it would be ready in 1 - 2 months, versus the one we were looking at in Rochester Hills, which was at least 3 - 4 months away from being finished. We were living in a small two-bedroom short-tem rental in a large apartment complex in West Bloomfield, and we dreaded the thought of having to be there with a small baby for 3-4 months. Plus, we thought it would be better to be around people who worked for a lot of different companies as opposed to primarily for Chrysler.

In the beginning going into the office was really strange, and it felt like a chore. International, along with the rest of the company, had just moved into the company's new World Headquarters at 1000 Chrysler Drive in Auburn Hills. The 4.4 million square foot facility was magnificent and a true testament to Iacocca's vision. Too bad he never got to spend time there. International was on the 9th floor in the tower. I was in the standard size cubicle for a grade-band 94 as opposed to the nice office I had in Paris. Everything was new to me, and at times I felt so out of place. Phil Bates, who I knew from SHAP, was responsible for putting the numbers together for the weekly and monthly sales and inventory reports, saw that I was lost and befriended me. He and I would go to lunch together. Phil was dealing with a lot of excessive aged inventory that we had from over-building units for certain markets, including some RHD vehicles. Tom had given me the assignment of working with Phil to see if I could identify sources outside of the dealers we could use to dispose of the vehicles. One problem was that most of the vehicles had been homologated to meet the unique requirements of the markets they were ordered for. In my research, I came up with two options. We could sell them to reputable wholesalers, which could be tricky, or sell them directly or indirectly to NGOs (Non-Governmental Organizations).

Selling to wholesalers was problematic and risky in that you could not guarantee where the units would end up, and whether dealerships would be available to service and repair the vehicles. One of the last things you wanted to have occur was to have a wholesaler sell vehicles into a market where you already have a distributor. The other problem is having vehicles in countries or locations without the ability to service or repair them. This could result in a sizeable number of abandoned vehicles thus creating the perception that the vehicle is of poor quality. No matter how strenuous the agreement with a wholesaler restricting where they can or cannot sell vehicles, it's almost impossible to enforce. When wholesalers buy vehicles from you, they want to turn them as quickly as possible and whoever comes to them with money, they will sell the vehicles to regardless of any limitations placed on them.

The second option of selling to the NGOs offered greater potential and less risk. Many of these organizations, such as the United Nations, Red Cross, WHO, UNICEF, The World Bank, Doctors Without Borders, Catholic Relief and companies like Halliburton and Bechtel purchased hundreds and thousands of vehicles. For us this was an untapped market with tremendous potential. It could be a source for disposing of excess inventory as well as generating new orders. None of our existing distributors or U.S. dealers would go after this business, because their agreements restricted them from selling vehicles outside of their designated geographical area of responsibility. The trick for us as a company, to avoid conflict with the existing distributors, was to make sure the orders were generated through their U.S. Operations and drop-shipped to their in-country locations. In the process of figuring out how we could pursue this opportunity, I discovered a company in Fort Lauderdale called Bukkehave that supplied vehicles and spare parts to the United Nations, NGOs, and companies. The company, which was 80 years old, was run by a young man named Christian Haar. We entered into an agreement with them to act as our authorized Chrysler, Jeep and Dodge distributor in developing countries. I also uncovered an organization called IAPSO, which is the international version of the GSA. IAPSO is the Inter-Agency Procurement Services Office; they assist UN agencies and development projects in purchasing goods and services.

While working for Tom was less than ideal, I was at least being productive. We both knew that my position in his organization was temporary, and that I needed to land something that was more permanent. One potential area was the Fleet department. The Fleet organization accounted for anywhere from 20-30 percent of the corporation's total sales depending on the need. The Vice President of the Fleet organization was Bill Glaub, who was considered a mover and shaker in the company. When I was in Paris, several U.S. headquartered Fortune 500 companies with offices in Paris, contacted the distributor Sonauto, wanting to leverage the Fleet purchases made by them in the U.S. They wanted to use those purchases to get higher incentives on the vehicles they were considering buying in Europe. They wanted to know how many more incentive dollars they would receive if they not only purchased vehicles from us in the U.S. but also in Europe. They were looking to leverage their volume.

Tom arranged for us to meet Wayne Snyder, who was Bill Glaub's second in command, to see if they had been approached by any of their multi-national customers with similar questions and to find out how they were handling it. In the meeting, we learned that the question came up a lot and that in a few cases, they allowed the vehicles purchased in Europe to count toward reaching their required purchase volume, but not as payers. Wayne shared with us that Ford was working on a program that was going to be a lot more comprehensive. The program being developed was going to consolidate their purchases worldwide and pay based on a global versus U.S. objective. To remain competitive he acknowledged that Chrysler was going to have to do the same. The problem was they did not know how to structure the program or understand the Fleet business outside of the U.S., which is where I came into the picture. I was transferred to the Fleet Department reporting to Bill Glaub. The Fleet group was housed at the American Center building in Southfield, Michigan on the 23rd floor, as opposed to at world headquarters in Auburn Hills. I was given an office with a door, versus a cubicle, and privileges in the Executive Dining Room at the top of the building. One of the first things I did in my new position was to arrange a trip to France with Bill Glaub and Wayne Snyder as part of an effort to acquaint them with the Fleet business in Europe. I could tell from watching Bill's reaction that he was being bitten by the international bug. He later became the President of Chrysler Canada.

My repatriation was far from ideal but in the end I landed on my feet. It took leveraging what I had learned and using it to create real value for the company. I was back in the rat race looking for my next promotion. On the personal side, once we moved into the house Rita could begin to establish a new norm for us and help work our way back into the swing of things in the U.S. She quickly made friends with our neighbors and reconnected with old friends in Detroit, we had lost contact with. She also went back to work after finding someone to take care of Danielle during the

211

daytime. Danielle had the easiest transition of all of us. For her, it didn't matter whether she was in Paris or Detroit as long as she was being loved and fed, and her diaper was clean.

#

Returning home to the U.S. was extremely difficult both personally and professionally. I was a different person ready to play a bigger part on a much larger stage. I was ready to move forward and become the leader I thought I was being prepared to be. Instead I felt like a caged eagle, ready to soar and with no place to go.

Jeremiah 29:11: "For I know the plans I have for you, declares the Lord, plans for welfare and not for evil, to give you a future and a hope."

Home Purchased in Michigan

DaimlerChrysler, the Merger of Equals: Yeah Right!

I just want to go on record as saying the "Merger of Equals" between Daimler and Chrysler, the biggest farce in modern business times, would have never happened if Lee Iacocca and Bob Lutz had been able to put aside their differences. If the baton had been passed to Bob Lutz (the heir apparent) and not to Bob Eaton, the merger would have never taken place. I don't think for a second that Juergen Schrempp could have convinced Bob Lutz that this was going to be anything less than a total takeover. In the streets, there is a saying that "game recognizes game", meaning people who are evenly yoked or equal don't try to deceive each other. If we look further into the rationale behind why Bob Eaton felt the need to pursue the merger, it was based on the fear that Chrysler needed a partner more so than GM or Ford to survive long term in the race toward globalization/consolidation. As much as the business world was talking about it, most of us didn't really understand what it would look like nor have a real model to work from. In simple terms, from my perspective, globalization or consolidation could be defined as having a wide enough presence/footprint to offer seamless market and product coverage as well as having the ability to leverage procurement worldwide and derive the greatest possible manufacturing efficiencies and cost benefits. I question whether a merger was the only way this could be achieved. The other possible options included strategic acquisitions, alliances, or partnerships. The problem is, this deal was ruled more by fear on Chrysler's part than foresight, and involved possibly a little greed. In this case, acting in fear caused the one thing we should have been most afraid of to happen and that was being taken over and losing our way. More foresight and insight would have caused us to consider other alternatives and not be taken in by the myth that you can have a merger of equals.

214

In May 1998, I was working in the Fleet department as the Senior Manager of Global Fleet Sales reporting to Christine Cortez, Vice President of Fleet Operations. Chris replaced Bill Glaub after he was promoted to the President of Chrysler Canada. It was an exciting time for me because I was working for someone I truly respected, who recognized and fully appreciated my abilities. The general mood in the company was good; it was a high point for Chrysler with respect to record profits and a string of successful product launches. Chrysler Corporation was the most profitable automotive producer in the world. The risk that we had taken in producing bold innovative vehicles like the Jeep Grand Cherokee, the LH sedans and the Dodge Ram, which captured the imagination and the spirit of the American buying public, had paid off. By the end of 1997 our market share had climbed to 23 percent, and our supplier relationships were the envy of the industry. Simply put, we were on a roll.

I think few executives in the company, outside of those that were involved in the deal, saw the merger coming. I am sure that like me, they were just as shocked and proud as I was when I first heard the news. It didn't take much for me to convince myself that we must be special, if a company like Daimler chose us to merge with and considered us an equal. It was like being picked by the prettiest girl in your high school class or, if you were a girl, by the school's biggest jock. I remember being summoned by Loretta, Chris Cortez's secretary, to the conference room with the other bonus role staff members for what we were told was going to be a major announcement. I didn't know what to think. My first thought was, could it be for Chris to announce she was being promoted to another area? Although she had been with us for only a short time, Chris was well thought of and considered to be on the fast track. When she announced the merger and shared the few details she had at the time, everybody was completely shocked and surprised. The rumor mill, which was pretty active in Chrysler, completely missed this one. Of course everybody had lots of questions and

215

unfortunately there were few answers available at that point in time. Right after we were told, she called in the rest of the Fleet staff to announce the merger to them. Over the next couple of weeks the rumor mill was working overtime. There were all sorts of speculation about why Chrysler, and questions about how this merger of equals was going to work. All we knew was that the short-term goal was to generate $1.4 billion in synergies during the first year.

The following week at the staff meeting, we were told of a new system that was being implemented to identify and track the "post merger integration synergies," referred to as PMI Synergies. Each area in the company was asked to begin a dialogue with their Daimler counterparts to identify ways that, working together, they could generate savings or incremental revenue. After identifying the various ways, you were required to determine the dollar value of the savings or revenue and put the information in the system. The system would be used to determine the total potential savings and revenue and to track the actual savings and additional revenue. I was advised by Chris that the person who headed up Fleet for the Mercedes passenger car group was a guy named Matthias Wuppermann. She also gave me the name of the persons responsible for Fleet at Freightliner, Sterling and M-B Commercial vehicles. She wanted me to contact the Mercedes passenger group first and set up a meeting. We could meet them in Germany, or they could come to the states. Her preference was to have them come to the states because their Fleet group was much smaller than ours. I made the contact and set up the meeting to take place at our office. For some reason, at the last moment Matthias could not come, but he sent the rest of his team. His team consisted of Jens Israng, Thomas Kokemore and Peter Bucheler The agenda for the meeting consisted of the following five topics of discussion: (1) Parameters and framework for working together. (2) Daily Rental opportunities. (3) Multi-National customer opportunities, i.e. potential joint Fleet actions and initiatives. (4) Benchmarking and comparison of different organizational models in use. (5) PMI Synergies. The meeting went extremely well, and we were off to a good start. The next meeting was scheduled in Stuttgart so that we could meet the rest of their team.

Because everybody was so cost-conscious, the trip to Stuttgart was limited to include myself, Frank Stephens, our Remarketing Manager and Mike Zdonek. Mike was responsible for Fleet sales in Europe based out of our European Headquarters in Brussels. During this meeting, we had the opportunity to meet Wuppermann and what a surprise that was. He was a German version of Fred Cody. He had a horrible temperament and a bad disposition. He didn't agree with any of the things we had agreed on in our meeting in Detroit. It was like starting all over with a new agenda, with him dictating the parameters. Jens sensed the tension that Matthias was creating and politely suggested that he might want to get back to more pressing things he had to deal with and let us continue working through the details. He assured Matthias that he would have him come back during the final review and wrap up, to get his final input. It became obvious during our second meeting that there was no way that working together we could garner savings by reducing cost. The only other way we could add to the PMI Synergies was to find ways to achieve incremental revenues. That meant one of two different things: we could generate conquest sales (new business) or regain lost business. It was also made clear that offering customers additional incentives on Mercedes passenger vehicles was not going to happen. They maintained tight control on the supply and demand of their products to avoid unnecessary incentives, they believed would diminish the brand. We left the meeting with the understanding that the Chrysler group would come up with a list of 10-15 commercial accounts that we felt we could conquest or regain by offering them access to Mercedes-Benz passenger vehicles for their top executives. The Mercedes group was to come up with 5-10 European accounts; they could leverage their relationship with to give us access.

Although much effort went into identifying potential customers and working out the structure for potential deals, nothing significant came of the initiatives. Most of our customers were expecting greater availability of their passenger cars at a better discount, which was not going to happen. Their customers were expecting them to use their influence to get us to give them bigger discounts than they were entitled to, based on the volume of their Fleet purchases. A lot of other areas in the company were having similar problems finding real synergies, which led to the decision that we needed to drastically cut cost. The decision to cut cost dramatically was met with extreme resistance, because the target for severe cost cutting was aimed at the Chrysler group and not at Mercedes the excessive and bloated side of the house. We were already a lean organization and were now facing the threat of further cuts. The culture clash had already reared its ugly head, and now the gloves were off.

The more we worked with our counterparts from Mercedes the more it was beginning to look like an acquisition than a merger of equals. We went from being the prize, to them being our savior. We saw one top officer after the other leave the company starting with Ted Cunningham, followed by Francois Castaing, Tom Stallkamp, Jim Holden, Sham Rushwin and Chris Theodore to name a few. Many of them were replaced by Germans such as Dieter Zetsche, Wolfgang Bernhard and Joe Eberhardt. Once we got over the notion of this being a merger of equals and accepted our position, it became a little less confrontational. Before we thought our opinions mattered and were quick to voice them. Now we had to be more careful and political. This was particularly difficult for many of the Caucasian males who ran Sales and Marketing. They were no longer in charge calling the shots, and they did not like the guy who was, Joe Eberhardt. He came in imposing many European ways of doing business.

They were uncomfortable with many of them, such as implementing target agreements. In Europe, each business unit was required to prepare and sign an annual target agreement detailing their sales volume objectives and inventory requirements. The combined target agreements would roll up into the Sales and Production forecast for the group. In the U.S., we generated similar annual forecasts with the difference being that on a monthly basis you could revise your forecast; it was not etched in stone. In their world, your target agreement commitment was etched in stone and could not be changed. You were expected to make the necessary changes in your organization to make your numbers. Achieving your Target Agreement meant everything in their organization. One key distinction that needed to be kept in mind is that Mercedes never over-produced vehicles; they always stayed shy of the projected demand curve. The U.S. mentality was that you will have to find a way to sell what you built, and what got built was based on the profit forecast.

The reality is that we were two unique companies with too many differences to successfully become one company. Our brands, which shaped much of our sales and marketing philosophy, were positioned totally opposite of one another. Our German and American cultures were too dissimilar to avoid the inevitable culture clashes. Even if Daimler had called it what it was, 'an acquisition', and we agreed to it, I don't think it would have worked. It was a bad idea doomed to failure from the beginning.

#

Relationships and agreements born from lies and deceit are doomed to failure. As much as we wanted to believe that things would be different it was hard to shake the feeling we were being lied to and that this merger of equals was too good to be true.

In 1 John 4:1, it says, "Beloved, do not believe every spirit, but test the spirits to see whether they are from God, for many false prophets have gone out into the world."

Deuteronomy 22:9-11 says, "You shall not sow your vineyard with two kinds of seed, lest the whole yield be forfeited, the crop that you have sown and the yield of the vineyard. You shall not plow with an ox and a donkey together. You shall not wear cloth of wool, and linen mixed together.

Out of Nowhere Came the Great Betrayal

A betrayal coming from a trusted friend or colleague is painful enough, but nothing can begin to describe the pain when it involves your only son and your brother. The spring of 2001 is a time I will never forget, because two of the worse things that could happen to you, happened to me. I don't want to make this all about me; I am sure it was equally if not more painful for the two of them. The difference was that the pain and disappointment they felt was the result of their own doing, and mine was from simply loving them.

When it happened, my son Richard was 33 years old. He was in the prime of his life, working for a Fortune 500 company he had been with for two years as a Credit Analyst earning $45,000, and I was so proud of him. Before I begin talking about the great betrayal, I need to get you caught up on my relationship with my son. In the beginning, it took me a while to step up and assume my responsibility as his father. Richard and his mother lived with his grandparents in a home they owned on 104th Street in Chicago. In the early years, I was around but not on a constant or consistent basis. I attended a few of the obligatory functions, but it wasn't until he was in high school that he and I began to have a closer relationship, albeit not a good one. Like most children whose father was absent from their life, he was angry with me and could not understand why I had not taken a more active role in his life. There was no way to explain the unexplainable even though I tried. I resigned it in my head and heart that only time together would make his pain go away, and hopefully as he got older he would understand.

In high school Richard was not a particularly outstanding student, not because he couldn't do the work, but simply because he was not focused enough and always made excuses. In June 1982, after graduating from 8th grade, he was scheduled to go to Corliss High School on 103rd and Corliss. At the time, I was living in Detroit working for Volkswagen and married to Allean. Because of the gang problems at Corliss, his mother at the last minute decided to switch him to Simeon Vocational High School. He went there for a year or so and then transferred to Morgan Park High School because he wasn't doing well, and they thought he would do better at Morgan Park. In his junior year, he got into trouble at Morgan Park for smoking marijuana and was kicked out of school. Of course he denied it and said the teachers had it in for him. His mother decided he needed to get out of Chicago and sent him to Piney Wood, a boarding school for African-American kids located in Piney Woods, Mississippi. The school recognizes that there are African-American students who have the capability of leading extraordinary lives through excellence in education and the development of moral and ethical attitudes, but do not have an opportunity to do so for various reasons. Piney Wood's mission is to provide that excellence in a Christian manner. After learning more about the school, I thought it might not be a bad place for Richard. I hoped being in a structured and disciplined environment would make a difference. It wasn't long before he got kicked out of Piney Wood for trying to smuggle marijuana onto the campus. Once again, he denied it was he and instead insisted it was his roommate, who was also from Chicago. They were both sent home. When he returned back to Chicago, he went to Percy L. Julian High School, which is where he eventually graduated from in 1986.

After graduating from high school he headed off to college at Iowa State. I was shocked to learn that instead of staying in a dormitory on campus, which most freshmen are required to do, he was staying on campus in an apartment by himself paid for by his mother. Like most kids away at school, he had a hard time allocating his time between hanging out and hitting the books. By his sophomore year, it was obvious he was having problems academically. I got a long letter from him telling me that at the end of the summer session, he would no longer be attending Iowa

State University. He indicated he was considering enlisting in the Air Force National Guard, in the fall. After completing his service in the National Guard his plan was to continue his studies in electrical engineering at Howard, Hampton or the University of Illinois. Then he was planning to go to the University of Michigan to participate in their MBA/Law Degree program. Of course none of this happened; instead that summer he moved in with his friend Butch. He later returned to Chicago and moved in with his mother (who was recently married) and her husband.

Over the next couple of years, from 1990 to 1992, Richard spiraled in and out of drug rehabilitation programs, trying to get himself together. I don't know the full depth of his drug addiction, but I have heard from others that it was pretty bad. During a lot of this time he and I were estranged because I could not stand all the lies and deceit. In 1992 he got himself together with the help of Drug Addicts Anonymous and enrolled in Olive-Harvey College, a junior college on the South Side of Chicago. He was saying all the right things, but I wasn't sure he meant it. I decided to try our relationship again, but with extreme caution. He was committed to getting his education and ended up on the Dean's List and receiving an Associate of Arts degree from Olive-Harvey on May 13th, 1994. In order for him to apply to a four-year college or university, he had to pay off $6,575.19 owed for a Guaranteed Student Loan to the Iowa College Aid Commission. In order for them to release his transcripts, which he needed to submit with his application, he had to agree to a payment plan of $160.00 per month and give them a lump sum payment of $1,310.00. He asked if I could provide the lump sum amount if his mother agreed to make the monthly payments. I told him I would consider giving him the money he needed, but he was going to have to make a formal request in writing. Since I viewed this as an investment in his education, I wanted to see in writing an investment plan detailing the investment opportunity and outlining the courses he planned on taking to get his bachelor's degree from Loyola.

223

He prepared his plan, which was spiral-bound and included his profile; the school of business curricula with all the requirements to graduate; an overview of all outstanding loans; a letter to prospective investors; copies of all of his grades from Olive-Harvey and letters of acceptance from Loyola University, DePaul University and the University of Illinois. Knowing that I was biased, I had him send a copy of his plan to Bill Adkins for him to review and provide me with his input. He was impressed with his plan and thought he was sincere. I gave Richard the money he needed, and he started classes at Loyola University in the fall of 1994.

Richard continued to remain drug-free and stayed focused on his studies. He was on the Dean's List at Loyola and in the spring of 1995, he applied to take classes at Loyola's Rome Center during the summer semester. He was accepted and took two classes in Global Business Strategy and Political Science at the Rome Center. He was proud of his accomplishments, especially being able to take classes at the Rome Center. He knew this was something I regretted not doing when I was a student at Loyola. He spent a month in Rome, which was a great learning experience for him. At the end of his stay in Rome he came to Paris to spend time with us. We traveled all around Paris, drove to Bruges, Belgium and took a vacation to Amsterdam. On May 11, 1996 he graduated from Loyola University with honors and a Bachelor of Business Administration degree, majoring in finance.

On his own he got a job after graduating, working for Chrysler Finance in their Collections Department. He was doing well staying out of trouble and dating. The only thing that concerned me was his lack of desire to assert his independence. You would think that after graduating from college, one of the first things he would do is move out of his mother and stepfather's home. He had a room in their attic and seemed content being there. When I questioned him about why he did not make an effort to get his own place, he would tell me that he was only staying there until he

224

could pay-off his school loans. It made sense logically, but he just seemed too comfortable living with his mother and not being on his own. A couple of years later he left Chrysler because he felt the opportunities for advancement were limited. In February 1999 he was hired by Kraft Food as a Credit Analyst.

Now that we are caught up, let's talk about what happened in the spring of 2001. In April 2001 Richard and I had been corresponding back and forth. He knew I was a little disenchanted about things at Chrysler and was considering other options. He thought it would be helpful if I could chat with one of their group Vice Presidents at Kraft whose responsibility included Marketing Services. He knew her secretary and was trying to set up a phone conference. My oldest daughter, Alyssa, was a junior in high school at North Atlanta High School. She was coming to San Francisco during her spring break to join me. I was in San Francisco for the Annual Fleet Week. She was coming out so that we could tour several schools of fashion and design in San Francisco. She wanted to visit the Fashion Institute of Design and Merchandising and the Art Institute of California. I also wanted her to visit UC Berkeley. My oldest brother Barlow, who lived in Marina Del Ray, California near Los Angeles, had been spending a lot of time in Chicago. In fact, he was staying with my mother-in-law. She had mentioned to my wife on several occasions that he was acting strange, and that she was worried about him. I asked Richard privately to check in on him to make sure he was okay. He reluctantly agreed to do so for me, because according to him, he did not like my brother. He told me he was too loud and flamboyant and bragged too much about what he had.

On Friday, April 20, 2001, when I was in San Francisco with Alyssa, I got a call from Richard telling me that my brother Barlow had been arrested in Columbia, South Carolina. He had been arrested and charged with conspiracy to posses and distribute cocaine, along with his girlfriend Regina Coleman. According to what I later learned from reading the local newspaper, they were arrested after one of Regina's girlfriends, Delores Glover from New York, was caught in Charlotte trying to sell a kilo of cocaine to an informant for the Department of Alcohol, Tobacco and Firearms. Delores agreed to lead them to her source, which she identified as my brother and Regina. The federal, state and local agents, armed with a search warrant, kicked in the door at Regina's home in Northeast Richland at 8:00 p.m. on Thursday, April 5 and seized a kilo of cocaine, $320,000 in cash and some firearms. They found $220,000 in a jet ski in the garage and the rest of the money hidden in a blue cloth Crown Royal liquor bag in a box that held a 12-pack of Sprite. They were suspected of having sold anywhere from 30-50 kilos of cocaine. I was in complete shock when I heard this; I knew he was going down for good and would not be able to work his way out of this one like he had done in the past.

What I was not prepared for was what happened next. Richard wanted me to go to my brother's apartment in Marina Del Ray and get his things out of there. I didn't know what things he was talking about, but I assumed he meant money, clothing, shoes, furs and jewelry. When the shock of my brother being arrested wore off, my immediate concern was why he was asking me to go to my brother's apartment, and telling me that if I were scared he would do it. It wasn't about being scared. It was a matter of not wanting to get involved and put myself or my daughter at risk. He gave me the name of one of Barlow's friends named Gwen, who would help me get into his apartment. As I tried to think my way through all of this, I decided I was not going to drive down to LA and meet Gwen. Doing so would mean getting Alyssa involved in this in some way, which I was not going to do, and how would I ever be able to explain it to her mother, if something happened. Secondly, I reasoned that the authorities by now could be watching his apartment, although Gwen assured me they would not have acted that fast. When I asked her why she didn't go do it, she said they would not let her into his apartment, but would let me because I was his brother. I told her no and then proceeded to tell Richard that he shouldn't go either.

I slowly began to shift from being shocked to feeling there was more to this story than I was being told. That's when I proceeded to ask Richard a few of the questions that had been running through my mind, but that I had blocked momentarily, while I tried to absorb all of this. First I wanted to know how he knew, Barlow had been arrested. Secondly, how did he know what my brother had in his apartment and about Gwen? Lastly, why was he so concerned about somebody he said he didn't like? He explained to me that after I asked him to check on Barlow, he hung out with him a couple of times and discovered he wasn't as bad as he originally thought he was. He then began to call him every now and then to check up on him, which is how he had his number to give to Gwen. He claimed he knew what he had in the apartment because that's what Gwen told him. She told him that he had all of those things in the apartment, including a lot of money in a safe. His explanation was plausible but there was this strange feeling in the pit of my stomach. I used to jokingly say whenever his lips were moving, he was lying and that's how I was feeling at that moment. As for the things in Barlow's apartment, someone crawled through the ventilation system and dropped down through the vent in the ceiling and cleaned out his apartment.

Still reeling from the news about my brother, two weeks later on Thursday, May 10th, I got a call from Richard's girlfriend, Carolyn. She told me that he was in jail, and that he had been busted by the FBI. She said she didn't have any more information than that to give me. Once again, I was in a state of shock and didn't know where to turn. I suddenly remembered the names of two guys I went to high school with Kenneth Payne and Sam Lemon, who worked as undercover narcotic detectives at the police station on 51st and Wentworth, near the Dan Ryan. I contacted Kenneth and asked him if he could look into this for me. He called me back and told me that Richard had been arrested in a sting operation trying to sell 250 grams of cocaine to an undercover FBI agent, and that he was being charged with possession with the intent to distribute. He said that since it was a federal matter that there was nothing he could do to help. He did, however, give me the names of several attorneys that he knew that handled cases of this type. He strongly recommended that I first try reaching an attorney named Mike Gillespie located in downtown Chicago. He went on to tell me that they had Richard cold, and that the entire thing was taped and on camera, which would make it difficult for him to argue he was not guilty. When I contacted Mike Gillespie, and after he looked into the matter, he pretty much told me exactly what Kenneth told me about them having him on camera. To retain his services I was told it would be $5,000 to plead him out, which is what he would suggest doing, and if he wanted to plead not guilty and go to trial it could cost up to $25,000.

Over the weekend Richard called me from jail. Overwhelmed by recent events, all I wanted to know was why. I couldn't understand why someone who was college educated with a good job would be selling drugs. He kept telling me that was not important, and that he was innocent. He wanted to know if I had the $25,000 to pay the attorney. I had already sold stock from my stock portfolio to generate the $5,000 retainer the attorney required. I told him that I didn't have $25,000 to throw away to defend someone who was guilty, and that the FBI had on tape. He told me that if it was his son, he wouldn't question him, and that he would do whatever it took to raise the money. The more I talked with him the angrier I got. Here he was talking to me like I was an idiot, telling me what he would do, but unwilling to tell me why he did it. I left the conversation outraged by his attitude and decided it was time that he dealt with the consequences of his actions. I cut off all conversations and contact with Richard.

I later found out that Richard had been set up by a friend of his, Tony. Richard grew up with Tony, who had become a local drug dealer in the neighborhood. According to what I was told, Richard introduced Tony to his Uncle Barlow, who, he told him, was a big time dealer from California. Richard traveled with Tony to California to buy drugs from Barlow, and on the way back to Chicago, Tony got busted at the airport. Richard tried to get Barlow to help bail him out, but Barlow told him no, that he was on his own. Richard then took money from his 401K to bail Tony out. Tony was released from jail, and unbeknownst to Richard, was flipped by the feds and became an informant. He was the one who helped them set up the sting operation that took Richard down. I am sure all of this was done with the intent of using Richard to set up Barlow. Instead of using Richard to take Barlow down, which happened independently, they used Richard as a witness against him. As part of Richard's plea bargain deal he had to agree to testify against my brother, his uncle.

I did not speak to Richard until September 2007, a year or so after he was released from jail. We have since rekindled our relationship. I have not spoken to Barlow, who is scheduled to be released in 2037. The last time I spoke with him, he was bad-mouthing Richard and trying to convince me that I owed him and should send him money. I made it clear to him how betrayed I felt that he would get my son involved in his drug dealing. He told me Richard came to him and instead of sending him packing, he decided to teach him the ropes. He rationalized that it was better he learn from him than someone else who wouldn't have his back. How ironic that statement was. I told him that if his son had come to me, that there is no way I would do anything that would put him at risk. Somehow he could not understand why I felt this way. We exchanged a few more words and in anger, I told him that the next time we saw each other one of us would be looking down at the other one. I have not spoken to him since that exchange.

#

There is no greater biblical reference to betrayal than what you find in Matthews 26. It speaks of the day of the Feast of the Unleavened Bread and how the disciples came to Jesus asking where do You want us to prepare for You to eat the Passover. They were told to go into the city to a certain man and tell him the teacher says the time is near, and that He was going to celebrate the Passover with the disciples at His house. The disciples did as Jesus directed and prepared the Passover. When evening came while reclining at the table with His twelve disciples He said I will tell you the truth: one of you will betray Me. One by one they said "surely not me Lord." Jesus replied - it will be the one who has dipped his hand into the bowl with Me. He went on to say the son of the man will do as written about him, but woe to the man that betrays the son of man. It would be better for him if he had not been born. Then Judas, the one who would betray him said," Surely not I." Jesus replied, "Yes it will be you."

The betrayal by my brother and son is still a challenge for me. Like Jesus, I need to symbolically take the cup and drink from it then say to myself "this is the blood of the covenant which is poured out for many for the forgiveness of sins." According to Rev. Patrick O'Neill, Senior Minister, First Unitarian Church of Wilmington, Delaware, in a sermon he delivered on October 8, 2006, "Forgiveness is hard. It's hard to give. It's hard to receive. It's even harder to talk about. It is soul work on the deepest level. Despite all the practice, we've had over a lifetime of telling each other we're sorry for all the intentional and unintentional hurts and harms, we do in this limited living space together forgiving each other is hard.

If there is one fundamental misunderstanding about what forgiveness is and what it does, it is this: a lot of us still think forgiveness is something we give to other people, to people who have wronged us and who may or may not be sorry for what they did to us. But that is only part of the story, and it misses the true nature and power of this act of will. Forgiveness is first and foremost a gift to ourselves. It is an act of self-love, self-care, self-respect, self-healing. It is the permission we give ourselves to let go of the pain of the past so that it does not define us for the future. There is only so much room in the human heart and if all your heartspace is taken up with a collection of unforgiven hurts and the bitter resentments that you have never managed to clear out through forgiveness, then your heart is all occupied, unavailable when the good stuff comes along . . . ."

When the Wheels Came Flying Off

Working for a large company like Chrysler can be exciting and frustrating at the same time. For me the biggest frustration was not the work itself, but not being rewarded or appreciated for my hard work. I have always had a strong work ethic, and I never shied away from working long hours (if necessary) to get the job done. Working in the Fleet department, it was not uncommon for me to work 10-12 hour days and weekends. The only time that I can honestly say I was recognized and rewarded for my efforts other than being sent to Paris, was in July 1999 when I was promoted by Chris Cortez to a grade-band level 95. She knew how hard I had worked single-handedly on the globalization initiative. She also respected and appreciated the wealth of knowledge and support, I provided her. Unlike most of my other bosses, Chris understood what it meant to not be one of the "good ole boys." I honestly believe that if she had remained in command of the Fleet department that things would have been very different for me. In fact, prior to her leaving the Fleet department, she submitted my name to HR to participate in the company's "High Potential Diversity Candidate" program. The program was designed to identify high potential incentive comp level diversity employees who were rated as a "top performer" on their most recent performance review, and who were deemed as having the ability to go at least 2 -3 grade levels beyond their current level. Those individuals would have a skip level meeting with Tom LaSorda, the Executive VP of Manufacturing that was assigned responsibility for overseeing the diversity initiative. You were also assigned a mentor and in my case it was Ed Brust, the President of Chrysler Canada, who assumed the role after the untimely and accidental death of Bill Glaub in November 1998.

During the latter part of 2001, around November or December, a change in senior management was announced by Joe Eberhardt, the

Executive Vice President of Global Sales, Marketing and Service for DaimlerChrysler. Chris Cortez was moving to a new assignment to become the Vice President of Parts and Service and Ray Fisher was named the new Vice President of Fleet Operations (as her replacement), both reporting to Eberhardt. While I was sad to see Chris leave, I understood that the rotation was good for her career. Ray Fisher, who I didn't know much about, had previously been the General Manager, Sales and Service reporting to M. John MacDonald, Vice President of Sales and Service. Ray, whose uncle was a high level executive at Chrysler, joined the company in 1974 right out of college. He worked as an administrative trainee in the New York Zone Office and worked his way up the ladder. He held various positions in the New York Zone Office before becoming the Assistant Zone Sales Manager in the Syracuse Zone in 1982 and in Detroit two years later. His first job as Zone Sales Manager was in Milwaukee in 1986, and he was promoted in 1989 to the same position in Detroit, a much larger zone. Following Detroit he spent time as the Zone Sales Manager in Chicago. In 1996 he became the General Manager of Chrysler/Plymouth in March and in August; he was appointed GM of Dodge Car and Truck.

It was common knowledge among the domestic sales and marketing organization that when John MacDonald moved on he would more than likely be replaced by Ray Fisher. In fact, Fisher had been told by MacDonald that he was being groomed for the position. In April 1998, when Fisher became the General Manager of Sales and Service after being the GM of the Dodge Car and Truck Division Gary Dilts had just been promoted to Executive Director of Retail Strategies and Dealer Development. Gary, who was on a fast track, was later promoted to Senior Vice President of eConnect Platform Team in January 2000. In February 2001, instead of Ray Fisher becoming the Vice President of Sales, Gary Dilts was appointed Senior Vice President of Sales and Field Services. This created a lot of tension having Fisher as the General Manager of Sales and

Service reporting to Dilts, the guy who got his dream job. The decision to move him to Fleet was part of an effort to retain both men, who were seen as vital in keeping the dealers focused and sales on track. When Ray Fisher arrived at Fleet Operations, which at the time was located in the American Motors Building in Southfield, Michigan, he was dejected and acted like a man exiled to a nearby island.

In the beginning, he seemed friendly and eager to learn. It wasn't long after he arrived that he realized Fleet Operations was not a bad place to be. It had lots of benefits. He quickly learned that it provided a great deal of autonomy and that wining and dining customers was much more pleasant than calling on dealers, who were always trying to squeeze you for something. It wasn't long before he settled into the job and decided that it was a chance for him to make his mark and upstage Gary. During the entire time Chris was Vice President of Fleet Operations, she never brought in one single person from outside of the department. It was clear from the beginning that Ray intended to bring in guys he had worked with in the sales organization. Prior to his coming to Fleet, he had convinced Chris to hire Mark Bosanac to replace Lewis Scott, who went back into the field. Mark had worked for Ray in the Chicago Zone Office. He came in as a grade-band 94, responsible for sales volume planning and vehicle distribution. Mark was not easy to get along with and seemed to have all the answers before knowing the questions. He came in with the attitude that he was going to teach us how the retail sales organization did it and showed little to no regard for the fact that the retail organization dealt with dealers and not customers, who were not obligated to purchase vehicles from us. The next person he brought in was Frank Dankovich to be National Daily Rental Manager following Don Glenn's retirement. Frank was recently divorced and from Chicago. The last addition to his team was Keith Helfrich, who was brought in by Ray to replace Frank Stephens, who headed up vehicle remarketing. Frank Stephens was a grade-band 95 and

234

Keith was brought in as a grade-band 96. The responsibilities of the position were expanded to justify the higher grade level.

When Ray took over Fleet Operations, I was one of three Regional Commercial Fleet sales managers responsible for the eastern half of the country reporting to Don Glenn. Don Glenn had previously headed up Daily Rental sales, and his role had been expanded to oversee all Fleet sales (Government, Daily Rental and Commercial). Chris had wisely decided that while the Global Fleet initiative had potential, it was going to take a while before it would be realized. She felt my talents would be better served in one of the more mainstream Fleet sales functions. Commercial Fleet Sales accounted for 25-35 percent of total sales and were the most profitable. You couldn't ask for anything more mainstream. I had a total of (17) Regional Account Executives (RAEs) and Zone Fleet Managers (ZFMs) reporting to me. The Regional Account Executives called on Fortune 500 companies, and the Zone Fleet Managers called on the dealers and the state and local governments. It was an awesome task that I enjoyed and felt I was well suited to handle. Many of the Fortune 500 companies were interested in discussing the possibility of doing business with us globally and my background made me the perfect person to develop the parameters. Also, my presentation skills were exceptional and were frequently used to assist in the preparation of presentations for clients and large groups. The selling skills I lacked early in my career were fully developed, and I knew how to close big deals.

Working with my two other colleagues Bick Pratt, who was responsible for the Central Region and Mark Charlson, responsible for the West, we completely revamped the Commercial Fleet Sales organization. In reviewing how we did business we realized that the competition had a lot more Regional Account Executives in the field calling on Fortune 500 customers than we did. We also realized that the Zone Fleet Managers, we had assigned to the zones were being redirected by the Zone Sales

Managers they reported to on a dotted line basis and shared office space with to perform, non Fleet related tasks. We decided that instead of having the dichotomy and friction between the Regional Account Executives and Zone Fleet sales Managers to eliminate the ZFMs and make them all RAEs and realign the territories. Ray initially resisted making the change because of all the push-back he got from his Zone Sales Manager buddies he had worked with for years. In the end, he went along with the implementation of our recommendation. This allowed us to increase sales by 17 percent in a down market and to reduce travel-related expenses by 30 percent. I was truly enjoying my job and felt I was making a big difference.

As much as I wanted to be respected and appreciated by Ray, and have him regard me in the same way he did the guys he brought in, it never happened. He created an "us and them" environment, which was obvious to everyone in the organization. From the other Department Heads in the office to the field organization, everybody understood that the only opinions or perspectives that mattered were his, Mark Bosanac's, Frank Dankovich's, Keith Helfrich's, and later Pat Dougherty's. The problem with this was that none of them had the Fleet experience everyone else had. The average tenure in the Fleet Department of most, if not all the department heads (except me), and the field organization, was well over 20 plus years. It was insulting and demeaning to watch them, in some cases, disregard the wealth of knowledge and experience that had been accumulated over years. It was very difficult for me to accept this kind of treatment while keeping my mouth shut and being respectful. Being true to the person I had become, I voiced my frustration with the difference in treatment during a one-on-one meeting with Ray. Although the purpose of the one-on-one meetings was to afford you the opportunity to speak candidly, it was not well received or appreciated.

In August 2001, Ray reorganized the Fleet department. He brought me into his office and told me that I was being switched from the Eastern

Region Commercial Fleet Sales Manager to being the head of the Customer Support and Bid Groups. The Customer Service group handled all customer inquiries and the placement and tracking of customer orders. The Bid Group prepared all federal, state and local bids as well as placed and tracked the orders associated with the bids we won. In addition to overseeing these two groups, I was given responsibility for the Company Car group, which had been folded into Customer Service. The Company Car group performed the same functions for the more than 30,000 company cars in service. In my new position, I managed upwards of 500,000 vehicles. According to Ray, I was being put into this newly consolidated position because they needed someone who could manage the details and turn-around the customer service situation. During the most recent industry conducted customer service survey, we had been rated the lowest of the big three. In addition to these changes, the Fleet Department was relocated from the American Center building in Southfield to world headquarters in Auburn Hills. Ray was eager to get back in the game and rejoin the rat race.

I just knew that with all the added responsibility, which included managing 50-plus employees, I was being promoted to a grade-band 96 and becoming a Director. The person I was replacing, Gerry Bergmoser, who was retiring, had been a Director and didn't have responsibility for company cars. The Company Car group previously reported to Don Glenn, who was also a Director. In spite of the overwhelming rationale for the position to be a higher grade-band, Ray assured me that he had tried but was unsuccessful in getting it done. He indicated that the company was reducing the number of grade-band 96s by replacing some of the ones retiring with grade-band 95s. What I discovered later was that Mark Bosanac had been promoted to Director of Market Development and Sales Planning, and that Joe Gholston was promoted to a Director level position handling all sales other than Bid. I couldn't shake the feeling that I was being taken advantage of, and being handed a scenario for failure by Ray. Somehow he found a way to get everybody else promoted except me.

Like many other times in the past, when I was handed lemons, I made lemonade. I took it as a challenge and opportunity to show the depth of my abilities. I conducted an assessment of each group and identified the necessary changes to achieve the goals that I had been given. What I found was that my direct reports were smart and capable. All they needed was leadership, support, and someone to stand up for them, which I was more than willing to do. Lou Amicucci, who was in charge of the Bid group, had worked in the group for more than 20 years. He came in every morning at 5:00 and knew more about the Bid business than anyone else. The Customer Service group was co-managed by Chet Kozlowski and Kathy Galanti. Neither Chet nor Kathy were demonstrative and lacked credibility with the customers and their direct reports. I knew I was going to have to make changes with both of them. Chet I would more than likely have to replace, and Kathy, who had been demoted from a grade-band 94 to a 93, needed constant reassuring and boosting for her confidence. Over time, I could reverse the situation with the Customer Service group by improving the level of customer communications, and visiting with the large leasing companies more often. I also let Ray talk me into replacing Chet with Lisa Way, which turned out to be a good thing. Regarding the Bid group, I immersed myself in the process and became a strong champion for the products we needed to successfully bid. I built a strong relationship with the GSA (government), and won their respect and ultimately was viewed very favorably by them. In fact, one of my achievements was that I secured the fourth largest single-source contract awarded that year, to provide Minivans to the Postal Service. The contract was worth $221 million. On the company car front, I became heavily involved in improving the level of customer service, we provided to our internal customers, and was instrumental in favorably changing the eligibility rules for company cars.

After struggling, and working an unprecedented number of long hours to significantly improve the groups I had been given responsibility for, Ray once again decided to throw me a curveball. He was convinced that we were not getting our fair share of the government business. Gary Dilts, who became his boss in December of 2003, had been telling him that there was a lot more business to be had. Gary's sister Donna was the Commissioner of the GSA in Washington and the basis for his comments. Somehow, Gary thought that if we had someone in Washington permanently, we would get more business. He kept harking back to the days when Gerry Bergmoser worked out of the Government Affairs Office in Washington, and that during those days our GSA volumes were much higher. What they refused to accept was the fact that the product specs had changed considerably, and included a lot more additional content that the GSA did not want and was unwilling to pay for. He and Ray concluded that I should be working in Washington and not Auburn Hills. Ray wanted me to move to Washington and hire someone to pursue Military Sales. He also had decided to take a portion of the Regional Account Executives and devote them exclusively to pursue the state and local Bid business. He took away my Customer Service and Company Car responsibilities and gave them to Lisa Way. I was given new volume objectives and told to select eight Regional Account Executives to be redeployed as Government Sales Managers (Gov's) to form my new team.

It took several meetings and phone conversations with management from the GSA to finally persuade them that having me in Washington was not going to change the bid outcome. The GSA procurement process was highly regulated and could not be influenced by relationships or personalities. Repeatedly, they heard that the only way to improve our bid results was to build products that better matched their specs and price them accordingly. With Ray partially convinced that I did not need to live in Washington, I started the process of identifying which

RAEs I thought would be the best candidates to become Gov's. It was also made clear to me that certain RAEs (the high performing ones) should not be considered. In fact, I was given a list to choose from which consisted of either low performers or ones Ray did not necessarily care for. I was also given the option of selecting two Gov's for markets where there was no RAE from the District Sales Managers in the zones involved.

Shortly after I completed the selection process, and was convinced that I had put together a pretty good team, Ray wanted to meet with the group. During the meeting, he repeated the objectives and to my complete surprise and utter shock told them that if the objectives were not met within a year, there would be some serious changes made and that their jobs would more than likely go away. I could tell looking into their eyes that they were instantly afraid that they might not have a job a year from now. I immediately communicated back to Ray that if it was his objective to intimidate by fear, that he had achieved his goal. He immediately responded that he was just trying to establish accountability and not intimidate them. Upon reflection, he later decided to send them an email indicating that it was not his intention to intimidate them but to create a sense of urgency with respect to achieving their goals. What I found interesting was that he didn't feel the need to do this with any other group other than mine.

It was clear to me, and my colleagues, that Ray had it in for me. Whenever we had off-site meetings, which typically involved spending an entire day or two in meetings at his country club to deal with sensitive matters in brainstorming sessions, I always felt under attack. When one of his guys made comments for suggestions he listened attentively and encouraged them. When anyone else spoke out and especially me, he seemed irritated and tried to find ways to marginalize or discredit what we were saying. He did the same thing during our weekly Monday morning staff meetings. I would dread going to them because no matter how

240

prepared I was for them, he would have something negative to say. I can recall one staff meeting to which I wore a bow tie, which I typically reserved for wearing to church on Sunday. When I walked in a few minutes after everyone else was assembled, he looked up and said without thinking, "Who are you today, Louis Farrakhan?" I was completely incensed and without much thought replied, "If I were, you would have never made that comment." The meeting continued, albeit with a high level of tension.

The week the proverbial wheels came flying off in October 2004, I was busy trying to get things cleared off my desk so that I could leave for a scheduled trip. During that week, I had several run-ins with Mark Bosanac, whose office was right next to mine. For the past year and a half, I had been waiting for him to champion changes to the specs of key products (trucks, Minivans and sedans) that I needed to improve our bid results, which he had previously agreed to do. Ray understood the importance of having properly spec'd vehicles to improve our bid chances, yet he never came down on Mark the way he would have if I was not getting it done. One evening I was working late and so was Mark. He came into my office demanding some information that he needed from me for a report he had to get out. The information was in my stack of things to do, and it was my plan to email it to him before I left that evening. However, I didn't like the tone he was using and one thing led to another, and we had words. I basically communicated to him, I didn't appreciate always being rushed by him for information he needed and his total disregard for the product support we needed from him, which by the way, was his job to provide.

The next morning when I arrived there was a message for me that I had a meeting scheduled with someone in HR at 10:00 a.m. When I went to the meeting I was told they were aware of my unhappiness and frustration with my management, and that my management felt the same way. We discussed the nature of my unhappiness and frustration and concluded the conversation with the HR representative suggesting that I

241

take some time off with pay, so we can figure out where we go from here. It was also "suggested" that given my length of service, that the company might be willing to consider some type of early retirement package if we could reach an amicable agreement. Before leaving, I asked him point-blank whether I was being terminated, and he said no. We both understood that there was no basis for my being fired. However, we were at a crossroad, and something needed to be done. I was aware of many others, including Pat Smorra, who had reached a similar crossroad, and I knew what needed to be done.

I went home right after the meeting and on the way home I quickly concluded that I needed to take whatever steps were necessary to protect my family. Somehow instead of continuing to be overwhelmed by fear and anger, which was my initial reaction, I suddenly experienced calm and began to think clearly. On the way home I called a friend who had gone through a similar experience and got the name of an employment and discrimination lawyer. I hung up the phone and called the lawyer. I was able to set up an appointment for the next day. During my brief phone conversation with the attorney, he advised me that his firm had several successful lawsuits against Chrysler. I left the call feeling I was in good hands. When I arrived home, my wife was surprised to see me. She was visiting with her mother who had stopped by. I told her that we needed to talk. I told her what happened and reassured her that we were going to be okay. She became immediately angry, because more so than anyone else, she knew the long hours and personal sacrifices I had made working for the company. It took me a while to finally settle her down and to remind her that the God we served would not bring us this far to let us down.

It took a while and some very intense negotiating, but we reached a more than reasonable settlement with DaimlerChrysler short of going to court, that kept us completely whole and ensured my retirement.

#

From my last day in the office and throughout this entire ordeal I was guided by Psalm 37. I kept reminding myself not to fret because of evil men or be envious of those who do wrong because: "Like the grass they will soon wither and like green plants they will soon die away. I trusted in the LORD and did good so that I could dwell in the land and enjoy safe pasture. I delighted myself in the LORD, so He would give me the desires of my heart. I committed to doing it His way and trust in Him to make my righteousness shine like the dawn and the justice of my cause like the noonday sun. I waited patiently on Him and did not fret that men would succeed in their ways, when they carried out their wicked schemes. I refrained from anger and turned away from wrath. I believed that evil men would be cut off and that those who believed in the Lord would inherit the land. I took comfort in knowing that during times of disaster the righteous will not wither; in days of famine, they will enjoy plenty."

CHAPTER 5

THE NEXT PHASE

Ready or Not, Retirement and the Realities it Brings are upon Us

Most baby boomers like me were looking forward to retirement when they reached age 66. According to Social Security benefit guidelines, individuals born between 1943 and 1954 will not be able to receive full Social Security benefits until age 66. If you got lucky and did everything just right, maybe you could retire at age 62. In today's world if you are anywhere near the vicinity of age 55, retirement has now become a daunting reality. It does not matter whether you like it or not, or if you're ready for it. This being said, it is important to note that legally you cannot be forced to take early retirement. This simply means your employer cannot force you, as an older employee, to take an early retirement package. Early retirement plans are only legal if the employee is offered a chance to stay on while keeping things the same or retiring early under a plan that leaves the employee better off than before. In early retirement situations, the employee must also have a real choice to reject or take the offer, the early retirement offer must be in writing, and the employee must have 21 days to decide and seven additional days to revoke.

Even with this reality, many employers faced with difficult economic times and changing dynamics in the workforce looking to cut costs have resorted to strongly encouraging early retirements. In a study published by the Center for Retirement Research at Boston College, the researchers combed through profiles of 22,000 Americans and found that while money and health weighed heavily on retiree happiness, what mattered more was whether they had control over when they retired. Being forced out of the workplace before you're ready is, unfortunately, a reality many of us are likely to be faced with. A full 40 percent of the retirees polled by the

Employee Benefit Research Institute in 2003 (long before the economic recession officially started in December 2007) had to retire before they'd anticipated.

Like many other Americans, for me it came much sooner than I anticipated, planned for, or was ready to deal with. I was not psychologically ready for the transition. Working gave me self-esteem, a real sense of purpose and accomplishment. It made me feel productive. Retiring prematurely meant losing all of that, and the adjustment was not easy. However, when I looked at things financially, I was in good shape based on the three-legged stool retirement theory. My 401K was sizeable; I had a pension from DaimlerChrysler, and could look forward to the prospect of receiving social security. Besides all of that, I was in relatively good health, had equity in my house, and was young enough to start a second career, or so I thought. At the time it never entered my mind that my 401K would be decimated, or that I would go from having positive equity in my home to being upside down. Neither could I have predicted that Daimler would selloff Chrysler to Cerebus Capital Management. A company completely ill prepared to do the things necessary to return Chrysler to good health. Who could have imagined that Cerebus would in turn sell it to Fiat while emerging from bankruptcy? Or that retirees like me would experience higher healthcare costs and be faced with the prospect that if Fiat does not turn Chrysler around our pension as we know it today could be in jeopardy. Lastly, no one could have told me we would be in a recession with unemployment reaching 10 percent, or that I wouldn't be able to find a job with my extensive sales and marketing background. Who could have imagined that more than 6 million Americans would be out of work six months or longer?

For me, the journey to where I am today included a pit stop along the way during which time I tried my hand at being an entrepreneur. After a short-lived venture with former colleagues who were previously subcontractors to me in my last position with Chrysler, I decided to look at potential franchise opportunities. I am sure the first thought that came to mind was why not become an automobile dealer? Unfortunately, most of my thoughts of becoming a dealer had long come and gone. In the mid '80s, right after leaving Volkswagen, I had seriously pursued becoming a GM dealer. I had applied for their Minority Dealer Development Program and was approved. Part way through the process, I began to question the sincerity of the program when they kept trying to encourage me to consider dealerships in small towns, where the prospect of a minority dealer surviving was questionable. When I presented them with a dealership purchase opportunity in Chicago, which I thought would be perfect for me, they were unwilling to make negotiating the deal a priority. I was repeatedly told they had others ahead of me, and that I would have to wait for my turn. The other reason it was out of the question for me, is that I had watched Bill Adkins and his wife Pauline Adkins have their dealership, Planker Chevrolet, in West Babylon, New York taken away from them by GM. The Office Manager, which GM insisted he keep, committed fraud, embezzlement, and conversion by illegally diverting cars from the dealership's inventory to her friends and family and falsifying payoff documents. During the course of this, the books were repeatedly audited and certified by an accounting firm hired by GM to audit dealers in the program. In the end GM blamed him and held him accountable for all losses. They sued and won in the lower courts only to have the decision reversed on appeal. They were devastated when this happened.

In looking at potential franchise opportunities in 2006, I was made aware of a marketing related franchise opportunity by none other than Fred Cody, my former boss from Chrysler International Operations. Fred had been gone from Chrysler for more than 10 years. He was finally walked out of the door for his outrageous behavior during Tim Adam's tenure as the GM of International Operations. For the first couple of years after leaving

Chrysler, he spent time working for Lee Iacocca with his EV Global Motors electric bike project. He later spent time working on different projects at one of the two companies started by Rex Smith, formerly one of the VP's from Ross Roy, the marketing firm. He was now working as the Business Development Manager for the PRstore in Royal Oak, Michigan owned by Linda Davis and Jim Moore. Jim Moore was previously the Executive Vice President, Director of International for Bozell, who called on Fred at Chrysler. He and his wife Linda had purchased the PRstore Franchise, which specialized in providing quality marketing services to small and medium-sized businesses. Fred knew that I was looking, because throughout the years we kept in touch, in spite of how badly he treated me at times when we worked together at Chrysler. In fact, we had become good friends, which he did not have many of from the past.

After visiting Fred at the store and talking with Jim and Linda, I decided this was something I might want to pursue. I was very impressed with the concept as well as the design and layout of the store. I also knew from my own experience that small businesses did not have access to quality marketing services and definitely not at an affordable price, which is what the PRstore offered. Jim gave me the name of the founders - Mike and Kathy Butler as well as the name of the person in charge of franchising, Ira Distenfield. I contacted Ira, who, by the way, was also the owner of a PRstore in Santa Barbara, and we started discussing the prospect of me buying a PRstore. Ira was super friendly and a natural salesman. He was originally from Chicago like me and had worked for Mayor Bradley, the former mayor of Los Angeles. He and his wife Linda Distenfield had a store in Santa Barbara, which was doing extremely well, according to him. The store owned by Linda and Jim Moore was not doing anywhere nearly as well as Ira's, and they attributed it to the declining economy in Detroit given what was happening in the auto industry. Although I was impressed with Ira and especially the success he was realizing in his store, I had second thoughts about him because he made everything seem too good to be true. He also came off as if he was your best friend after knowing him for a relatively short period of time. I wrote it off to him being a good salesman.

During the course of my discussions with Ira, when I repeatedly asked to see numbers that would show me how the other stores were performing, he kept giving me the sales figures for his store and Mike Butler's store. At the time I was looking at purchasing one of the stores, they had stores open or in the process of opening in Grand Rapids, MI.; Royal Oak, MI.; Cleveland, Ohio; Woodland Hills, CA.; Sherman Oaks, CA.; Santa Barbara, CA.; Thousands Oaks, CA.; Charlotte, NC; Raleigh, NC; Memphis, TN and Louisville, KY. The explanation he gave for not providing me with the numbers was that most of the stores were just getting launched. Other than the store owned by Linda and Jim Moore, the remaining two or three stores were not doing well because the owners didn't have the kind of marketing background I had. He attributed their lack of performance to a combination of a lack of a marketing background and not following the formula the way he had successfully done.

Like any good salesman wanting to show you their product, Ira invited me to come see his store in Santa Barbara. Since I had seen Linda and Jim's store and spent time with them, I didn't see the need to go see Ira's store, instead I wanted to meet the founders. Ira arranged for my wife and me to meet the Butlers in Charlotte during a vacation trip to Myrtle Beach. Instead of meeting them at 'headquarters' we met them at one of Mike's stores located in the Bank of America high-rise building located in downtown Charlotte. I was not really impressed with the store itself, which was on the main level in what was once a sundry shop. I was told by the Butlers that it was a satellite location, which was the reason it was so small. Mike and Kathy (who went by KB) seemed to be nice people in their mid 50s, who had a strong background in marketing services and public

248

relations. During the meeting, they said all the right things, and we left the meeting feeling like they were old friends. I have since learned that people who befriend you too quickly bear watching.

Convinced that this had the potential of being a good deal the next step was to figure out where we wanted to open a store. My wife and I had decided that given what was going on in Detroit that we did not want to open a store in the Detroit Metropolitan Statistical Area (MSA), besides, Jim and Linda had purchased the franchise rights to the Detroit MSA. Ira had suggested on several occasions that Chicago would be a great location for us. My wife Rita quickly said no to Chicago because it was too cold, and she still had family living in Chicago that she did not want to have to deal with. She wanted to move someplace where it was warm, and we decided Atlanta. It was warm and we had friends and family there that we wouldn't mind spending more time with. Luckily for us, the Atlanta market was available. Unfortunately, it was only available because the person who originally purchased the franchise in Atlanta, who was a fairly young and avid jogger, died of a massive heart attack. Neither his wife nor business partner wanted to pursue opening the store after his death.

In March of 2006 I purchased the PRstore Franchise Rights for the entire Atlanta MSA. I paid for the first store and gave them a deposit to reserve the rights for the other seven stores, we determined the market could handle. My thinking was, I didn't want to put in all the hard work and effort to build the PRstore brand in the market and have someone else come in and reap the benefits. After looking at a number of potential sites for the first store in the Buckhead area of Atlanta, we settled on one on Piedmont and Lennox Road. It was a high traffic area with great visibility. In May, I packed up my things and moved to Atlanta. I found a furnished apartment on Piedmont down the street (within walking distance) from the store and began to complete the build-out process on the store and attend training in Charlotte. We had our official grand opening of the store in July. I had hired a young lady named Tiye Reese as a Marketing Consultant, who I thought had tremendous potential. She presented well and was creative. She also had good writing skills and was a whiz with the computer and anything technology related. She was just what I needed. The only downside was that she was the mother of three children, which periodically created challenges.

During the first 6 months of operations things were slowly coming together. However, I was not experiencing the kind of record sales that Ira insisted would be the case in a market like Atlanta versus, what he experienced during his first six months in tiny Santa Barbara. It didn't matter at the time because I was well capitalized and prepared for it to take a little longer before becoming profitable. In 2007, I could see things begin to turn the corner. I decided to hire a second person and after going through several employees, I hired James M. Dixon in May. James was a graduate from Florida A and M University with an MBA. I met him working as a waiter in Ron and Gladys Knight's Chicken and Waffle restaurant. He had moved to Atlanta from Virginia and was working there until he was able to find something else. I knew from his demeanor that he was more than just a waiter. He told me his background, and I asked him to give me a call. Several months later he did, and I hired him. Just as I suspected, he was a people person and had the kind of gift of gab that would allow him to sell anything. He was likeable and did a great job for me. By the end of 2007 my sales had me ranked third out of thirty-eight stores, right behind Ira Distenfield and Mike Butler.

In 2008 things changed not only with the economy, but also with the Butlers and their son-in-law Dan Fragen, who was the president of the company. Their focus went from doing things to ensure the success of the existing franchisees, to totally focusing on expanding the network (adding more stores). DesignCentral, which was responsible for the creative

250

development and production of all materials sold by the PRstores, became too bureaucratic and inflexible, plus the quality was questionable. The problem was that DesignCentral was run by KB, and nobody could tell her that things were not perfect. She kept her head buried deep in the sand. Customers complained that the proofs did not reflect what was in the creative briefs we were required to submit, and that the process of making changes to proofs took too long and was too bureaucratic. All KB wanted to hear was how great the design work was that they did. The reason the focus was on adding new stores was because it (the franchise fee) was an instant source of revenue for them, and they felt it was the fastest way to build up the company. The problem with that approach was that if you didn't correct the problems with the existing owners, it would ultimately impact your ability to attract new owners, which is exactly what happened.

At the height of their network expansion initiative, they had about 44 stores open. One by one the stores starting failing and their relationship with franchisees and employees deteriorated. Many of the store owners purchased their PRstores under-capitalized, because they had been told by Ira that they would be profitable in 3-6 months. In fact, he told one franchisee that was struggling to come up with the franchise fee to put it on their credit card, and they would be able to pay it off in two or three months. Under the best of circumstances, it would take at least a year or two to become profitable; not to mention we were in the throes of a deepening recession. Several owners lost everything, resulting in divorces and having to file bankruptcy. The staff at headquarters, which had grown to upwards of 30, one by one began leaving as they watched the behavior of the Butlers become more and more irrational. By the end of 2008 the level of dissatisfaction with the Butlers had reached a boiling point. People were openly admitting that they had been deceived and taken advantage of by the Butlers and Ira Distenfield.

Several owners independently filed lawsuits against the Butlers, and in April 2009 eight owners, including myself, filed a lawsuit against them. We hired a lawyer out of Michigan and tried to get around the provisions in the franchise agreement, which required going through mediation/arbitration in Illinois, and prevented us from filing a class action lawsuit against them. Pursuing them under the terms of the franchise agreement could end up costing each one of us upwards of $35,000, with no guarantee that we would be able to collect. Our attorney, in an effort to find a creative solution, recommended that we sue them for fraud and misrepresentation under the Racketeer Influenced and Corrupt Act (RICO). The lawsuit we filed in Michigan accused them of acts of omission that constituted violations of the RICO Act involving fraud and misrepresentation, as well as violations of the Michigan Franchise Agreement Investment Law and breach of contract, which resulted in economic damages to each one of us. Filing the lawsuit this way, which was a long shot, was our only way to get around the choice of law provision in the franchise agreement.

As things continued to deteriorate, we were notified in July that the court had granted the motion to dismiss filed by the Butlers' attorney in response to our lawsuit. Although we did not win the lawsuit, the reckless behavior of the Butlers, combined with the bad press and backlash from the store owners who did not participate in the lawsuit, caused sufficient damage to force the Butlers to file for Chapter 7 Bankruptcy on October 1, 2009. Mike Butler had closed his store a few months earlier. It was not long after that I made the decision to cut my losses and close my store. My decision to close the store was more a factor of the state of business in general, and not the loss of support from corporate. I had ceased using their services and found alternative sources long before we filed the lawsuit. It was a difficult decision but a necessary one.

#

My experience with the PRstore caused me to question why God allows bad things of this nature to happen to good people.

In Psalm 10 the question is asked: "O Lord, why do You stand off and hide Yourself during times of trouble? Because the wicked with all their arrogance lay prey to the weak or trusting who get caught in their lies and schemes. They boast of the desires of their hearts and praise greed while speaking evil of the Lord. Out of pride, they do not seek nor think about God. Everything they do profits them with no regard for Your laws, and they laugh at their enemies. They tell themselves nothing will hurt me and from their mouths they lie, curse and threaten. They lie in wait to ambush and murder the innocent and like a lion in cover lie in wait to catch the helpless. They leave their victims crushed under their own weight because they believe God has forgotten.

Those of us who believe know that the Lord hears the cry of the afflicted and knows their desires and will defend the fatherless, the oppressed and the wronged bringing an end to their fear."

PRstore Showroom

253

Finding Your Way Forward

Finding your way forward after early retirement is just as much about the spiritual journey as it is about the practical things you need to do. The first step is to conduct what I call the "Early Retirement Inventory Assessment" to determine where you are in your life both practically and spiritually:

- From the practical standpoint, do you have enough savings to live a reasonably comfortable life doing the things you enjoy?
- Is your pension secure; how many years are you away from being able to receive Social Security?
- Is your house paid for or how much more do you owe on it versus its current value?
- Can you be happy and fulfilled not being identified by your job or what you do?
- What do you want to do to fill your days?
- Do you have any unfinished projects or ambitions you want to tackle or pursue?
- Are there any organizations or causes you would like to devote some time to?
- What does your spouse want to do and how does that mesh with what you want to do?
- Where are you children in their life-cycle and what assistance do you anticipate needing to supply?
- Are your parents alive and what support do they need from you?
- Are you in good health and doing everything you can to be healthy?
- Do you have any hobbies or interests that could turn into a second career?

The other assessment you need to make is where you are in your spiritual journey. Many of us are at the very beginning of it and have a lot of work ahead of us and others are well on their way and will see retirement as a way of furthering their journey. To determine where you are, ask yourself the following questions:

- Do you know and understand the word of God and are you comforted by it?
- Do you have a personal relationship with our Lord and Savior that brings joy to your life?
- Are you obedient and do you follow His Will? Or do you struggle with understanding His will verses your own self-determination?
- Do you participate in acts of faith that He would be pleased with?
- Are your priorities' in line with your beliefs?
- Do you walk in faith or just talk about it?
- Are you active in church and community in the way you think He would want you to be?
- Have you taken control of your spiritual growth and journey by being in the driver's seat or are you a passenger along for the ride hoping you will eventually get there?

Retirement is about preparedness, knowing what you're going to do next both practically and spiritually. It's more than just having enough resources to survive to the end; it's having a plan and the spiritual fortitude to get you there. The people who have thought about it, made plans and embarked upon fulfilling their spiritual journey tend to get the most enjoyment out of it and are the happiest. Those who have not, need to start making their plans now because retirement can knock at your door sooner than you expect.

LaVergne, TN USA
27 February 2011
218063LV00001B/7/P